Northumberland
40 Coast and Country Walks

The author and publisher have made every effort to ensure that the information in this publication is accurate, and accept no responsibility whatsoever for any loss, injury or inconvenience experienced by any person or persons whilst using this book.

published by
pocket mountains ltd
The Old Church, Annanside, Moffat,
Dumfries and Galloway DG10 9HB
www.pocketmountains.com

ISBN: 978-1-907025-31-0

Printed in Poland REP2016

Introduction

'The English don't want us and the Scottish won't have us.' That phrase sums Northumberland's history up in a nutshell. For centuries the county was a bloody buffer zone between the two great nations. The important coastal town of Berwick-upon-Tweed has changed hands no less than thirteen times and the countryside was repeatedly burned and harried as armies marched over the ground and fired it into a smoking wasteland.

The Northumbrian people also waged war on themselves in organised violent family gangs known as the Border Reivers – the original Mafia. Think *Goodfellas* with leather jerkins and steel bonnets instead of Armani suits, Northumbrian accents instead of Italian and lamb stew instead of meatballs and tomato sauce.

The Robsons, Charltons, Fenwicks, Forsters and Milburns were just some of the prominent local Reiving families specialising in cattle theft, robbery and murder. They gave the words 'blackmail' and 'bereave' to the English language.

The Romans were the first to find the people of the area, who were then known as the Votadini, so difficult to control that they built a wall stretching from sea to sea in an awesome display of power and authority. There are also some that reckon Northumberland is where the famous Ninth Legion vanished. Their golden eagle standard is possibly out there somewhere, buried in a remote peat bog on one of the bleak purple hillsides.

The county has its own tartan, a black and white checked plaid known as the Shepherd's Tartan, and a small bagpipe that is played under the arm. The county flag of the independent, yet warmly welcoming people, features red and yellow stripes which you will see flying from many buildings.

Much of Northumberland is a National Park and the stretch up the north coast is designated an Area of Outstanding Natural Beauty. Hadrian's Wall is a UNESCO World Heritage site.

There is an abundance of wildlife that thrives in the tough wilderness of crags, moors, hills and valleys. The Farne Islands, just off the coast, are a sanctuary for 37,000 pairs of puffin and hosts one of England's largest grey seal colonies. There are also cormorants, gulls, terns, guillemots and razorbills on the grey, high exposed white guano-splattered rocks. You can pay the islands a visit on boat trips from Seahouses.

There is a herd of ancient wild white cattle at Chillingham, wild goats in Kidland Forest and the density of Kielder Forest has protected the native red squirrel population. Otters, badgers and foxes are all found in the county and there is the occasional 'big cat' sighting too.

The human population density is just 62 persons per square kilometre, giving the county the lowest population density in England. Plenty of space to think and walk here.

Northumberland is, however, packed with history and littered with castles and battlefields, as well as some of the best – and quietest – beaches in the UK. They would be ideal for beach soccer tournaments but for one thing – the climate. The cheerleaders' legs would go blue when a bracing breeze came whipping in off the cold grey North Sea!

That's something to bear in mind as you undertake the family-friendly walks in this book. It can get cold, wet and windy in the county, so remember to pack appropriate gear. Good walking boots will also help and a hot flask is always welcome. When the Vikings were charging off their longboats to terrorise the monks at Lindisfarne with battleaxes, they at least made sure that they'd come prepared.

There are five major long-distance walking routes in Northumberland – The Hadrian's Wall Path, The Pennine Way, St Cuthbert's Path, Northumberland Coastal Path and St Oswald's Way – as well as many days of excellent fell-walking in the rolling Cheviot Hills which straddle the border country. This book leaves those challenges to more experienced walkers; the routes that feature here don't aim to be feats of endurance, but refreshing daytrips that include some of Northumberland's finest points of interest and local history along the way.

While it is unlikely you will need an Ordnance Survey map for the easier

coastal walks in this book, for most routes – especially those in upland areas – putting one in your rucksack is advisable. The sketch maps provided are for rough guidance only.

If walking alone, you should also tell someone where you are going, what your route will be and when you expect to return.

Public Transport

While the main towns in this guide are all accessible by rail and bus, the starting point for some of the walks can only be accessed by car. Please remember when parking in rural areas to be considerate of people who live and work there and, in particular, take care not to block gates.

Countryside Access

Large areas of Northumberland National Park are accessible to the public as a result of the Countryside and Rights of Way Act 2000 (CRoW). This means that you can now walk freely on designated 'Access Land' without having to stay on rights of way. Up-to-date information about access land, where you can go and what you can do is available on the Countryside Access website.

Open Access Land across the National Park is clearly mapped on all the new Ordnance Survey Explorer Series maps, which were revised in time for the commencement of this new right.

Look out for the waymarking symbols that show when you are entering or leaving Access Land.

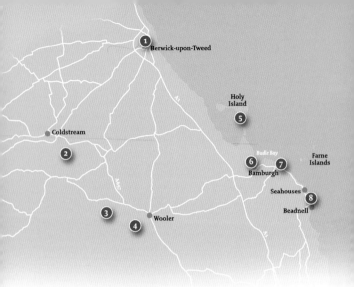

With its red-tiled roofs, fortified town walls and great bridges spanning the majestic River Tweed, Berwick is a great base for walkers wishing to experience the huge skies, wide beaches and rolling hills of north Northumberland. Things were not always so peaceful, however; Viking pillage and border warfare shaped this land and that bloody history features in many of the walks in this section.

Following a breezy walk around the walls of what was once Scotland's richest trading port, those with an interest in the history of relations with Northumberland's northern neighbour shouldn't miss the short tour of Flodden Field or the walk up Humbleton Hill near Wooler.

This area was home to people long before those battles, however, and a yomp up past the hardy goats on Yeavering Bell is well-rewarded with great views from the Iron Age fort at the top.

Down the coast, peaceful Holy Island (Lindisfarne) also has a bloody history; the monks here first saw the red and white sails and carved dragons of Viking longships approaching on the horizon in AD793. Today the tidal causeway stops it being overrun and it's a fascinating place to explore.

Further south are some of the finest beaches in England. Budle Bay is simply stunning and the coastal walking here is second to none. Any visitor to this area must also spend some time exploring Bamburgh and its glorious dune-backed beach. The last walk is from the quiet harbour at Beadnell, with the ruined walls of Dunstanburgh shimmering in the distance, to the busy port at Seahouses.

Berwick, Wooler and Bamburgh

Berwick Walls

Distance 4km Time 2 hours
Terrain tarmac and coastal paths with
some steps Map OS Explorer 346
Access car parking north of the town
walls; public transport by bus or train
to Berwick

Enjoy an easy stroll around a historic
garrison town that has changed hands
between Scotland and England some
thirteen times.

Berwick's ramparts were built between
1558 and 1570 to deter any attack from
French or Scottish forces, who were allied
at the time in support of Mary Queen of
Scots. The defences were never tested –
Mary lost her head and the crowns of
Scotland and England were united in 1603.

Park in the Castlegate (pay and display)
car park near the Scotsgate archway in the
shadow of the town walls. Go through the
archway and up the steps on to the
ramparts. Detour left for a superb view
over the Tweed and its impressive bridges
from Meg's Mount, once a platform for a

fearsome heavy gun known as Roaring
Meg, before following the ramparts to
Cumberland Bastion, keeping a tight rein
on children as there is a sheer drop off the
walls here!

The arrow-shaped bastions were
designed to provide as wide a field of fire
as possible; the cannon on the far side of
Cumberland Bastion demonstrates how
effective this defence would have been
when fully armed. The bastion, facing
Scotland, is named after The Duke of
Cumberland, known north of the border
as 'Butcher' Cumberland for his ruthless
treatment of captured Jacobites following
the Battle of Culloden in 1745.

Continue on towards the North Sea and
the Brass Bastion. Enjoy unspoilt views
out to sea from the top of the mount,
then carry on around the ramparts above
the Stanks football pitch, site of the
annual summer cup for local amateur
sides, and on to the Windmill Bastion.

Halfway between the two bastions is
the Cow Port, the only surviving original

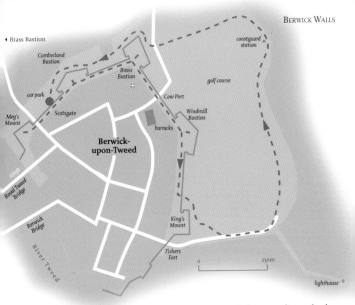

gate to the town. In 1318, Peter de Spalding, a local burgess with a grudge against the town's governor of the time, helped Robert the Bruce capture the town by leaving the gate's portcullis half raised.

The impressive square building to the right is Berwick Barracks, which was home to the King's Own Scottish Border Regiment between 1881 and 1964 and houses the regimental museum. A safe distance beyond the barracks is the Magazine, its thick buttressed walls designed to contain any explosions.

You can carry on along the walls here, for views over the mouth of the Tweed from King's Mount and Fisher's Fort (with a Russian cannon captured during the Crimean War at St Sebastopol), or take the steps down to your left and bear right. Carry on along the path to some houses, then take the steps to your right which lead down to the harbour.

Continue along the pier out to the lighthouse or turn left just before the cottages down a walled lane. This leads out to a small car park and the clifftop path; follow this round the golf course, watching out for stray balls.

Soon after you pass the coastguard station take the tarmac path through the golf course back towards the Brass Bastion. Follow the path at the foot of the ramparts as it swings left and leads you back past the Cumberland Bastion and on to the car park outside the Scotsgate.

9

Flodden Battlefield Trail

Distance 1.6km **Time** 1 hour
Terrain grass waymarked paths with
information boards, brief roadside walk,
steady ascent and descent **Map** OS
Landranger 74 **Access** car park at the
battlefield site just past St Paul's Church
in Branxton, roughly 1.5km west of the
A697, 16km north of Wooler and 6km
south of Coldstream. Infrequent buses to
Branxton from Berwick-upon-Tweed and
Wooler are run by Glen Valley Tours
(glenvalley.co.uk)

This short walk explores one of the best
preserved battlesites in Europe. The
Battle of Branxton Moor, or the Battle of
Flodden Field as it is better known, was
the last great medieval battle fought on
British soil and its repercussions were
felt for many years after.

The conflict arose when James IV
declared war on England to honour the

Scots' Auld Alliance with the French who
were fighting Henry VIII in Europe. Both
sides assembled massive armies and on
September 9th 1513 engaged in ferocious
battle. The smaller English army was led
by the Earl of Surrey, a battle-hardened
and brilliant tactician, who took full
advantage of weaknesses in the Scots
weaponry and miscommunication in their
ranks. It is thought that up to 10,000 Scots
were killed, including King James IV and
much of the Scottish nobility, with
English losses put at about 1500. The
defeat was catastrophic for Scotland and
changed the nation's history; it is said
that nearly every noble Scots family lost a
member at Flodden.

Park in the battlefield car park just
beyond St Paul's Church in Branxton and
head up the steps by the information
board. Bear left at the top of the steps to
visit the monument, erected in 1910, then

◄ Flodden Monument

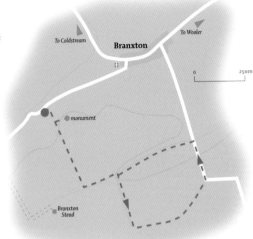

To Coldstream

Branxton

To Wooler

0   250m

● monument

Branxton
Stead

return to the wooden seat and follow the waymarker down the grass path by the hawthorn bushes at the edge of the field. At the bottom of the hill, cross the small burn and turn left through the metal gate, then follow the yellow waymarkers along the bottom of the next crop field to the wooden gate.

Turn right here, following the sign for the viewpoint uphill. At the information board at the top, turn left and take in the view of the battlefield spread out before you. Head along the grass track; at the next board you find yourself in what would have been the heart of the Scottish lines in a commanding position on the high slope looking down on the Earl of Surrey's army.

Keep going left to the edge of the field

and the next information board, then emerge onto the roadside, heading downhill towards Branxton.

Turn left off the road back onto the trail at the metal gate. Some of the most devastating fighting would have taken place here, on what was then very boggy ground. Many of the Scots soldiers took off their footwear and fought in their hose to get a better grip in the mud. The faint sound of the clash of steel, as well as screams and groans from that fated day are said to still be heard on some dark nights. Ghostly apparitions of soldiers are also occasionally seen crossing the A697.

Head back to the gate at the start of the trees and continue through, turning right onto the path up to the monument and back to the car park.

Yeavering Bell

Distance 5.5km Time 3 hours
Terrain farm tracks, grass paths, steady
ascents and a steep zigzagging descent
on a well-walked trail Map OS Explorer
OL16 Access car parking at Gefrin
monument lay-by on B6351 road, 8km
from Wooler or on grass verge just before
Old Yeavering. Do not obstruct track or
gateways. Nearest public transport is by
bus to Wooler

Yeavering Bell dominates the north
Cheviot foothills and the remains of the
settlement on its twin-humped top
make it the site of the largest hillfort
in Northumberland.

Start the walk from the cottages at Old
Yeavering and follow the path straight
ahead towards the often cloud-shrouded
hill. Bear right up the public footpath
signed for Hethpool – ignore the sign for

Yeavering Bell here – and continue on the
farm track by the yellow waymarker. The
ruined rectangular farm building here is
known locally as King Edwin's Palace;
there was once a tower near here and the
building's foundations are thought to be
much older.

Keep on the track by the fast-flowing
burn until you reach a waymarked turn-
off on your left for the Hillfort Trail.
Go through the five-bar gate and
continue up the trail as it swings by
the woods up to a laddered stile. This
part of the walk follows the St Cuthbert's
Way to Lindisfarne.

Bear right uphill, following the white
markers on the grassy path, and at the
ankle-high wooden sign turn left to head
across onto the hill itself.

Go through the bracken and heather,
following the regular markers, and cross

the burn to begin your gradual ascent as the track turns left. Look out for wandering feral goats on the hillside – Yeavering means 'hill of the goats' – and hawks hovering in the magnificent silence.

Head steadily uphill on the trail to the entrance of the Iron Age hillfort. The wall here was once 10ft thick and surrounded the two peaks of the hill and around 130 timber buildings, the largest of which was 42ft across.

Exit the fort at the back wall in the middle of the two peaks, following the regular waymarkers down to the left off the exposed top.

Carry on down the steep hillside of bracken, bilberries and loose scree, following the waymarkers to a stile and the track back to Old Yeavering.

On the way down you can look beyond the road end of Old Yeavering to the site of Ad Gefrin, the 7th-century palace of King Edwin, lost for centuries until identified by crop marks in 1949. The impressive monument by the B6351 stands by the side of the field once occupied by this important settlement. The large obelisk on Lanton Hill to the north commemorates a local landowner and is not connected to Ad Gefrin.

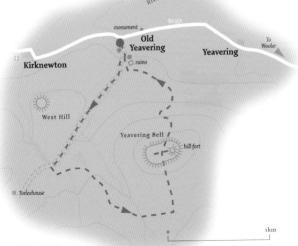

◀ Wild goat on Yeavering Bell

Humbleton Hillfort

Distance 4km **Time** 2 hours
Terrain grass paths, steady ascents and a
steep descent on a well-walked trail
Map OS Explorer OL16 **Access** car parking
on grass lay-by in Humbleton 1.6km
north of Wooler on the A697. Nearest
public transport is by bus to Wooler

Humbleton Hill is a quiet and peaceful
place today, but it was also once the site
of a terribly one-sided battle; the fields to
the north were so stained by blood that
they became known as Red Riggs.

In September 1402, a Scots army under
the command of the Earl of Douglas had
plundered the county down to Newcastle.
They were on their way home when the
legendary Harry 'Hotspur' Percy met them
just beyond Wooler. His archers let loose
from the opposite slopes of Harehope Hill
and with the sky black with arrows, the
Scots fell like dominoes. More than 800
were cut down and 500 more were said to
have drowned in the Rivers Till and Tweed
as they tried to get away. The English
claimed to have only suffered five
casualties. The Earl of Douglas, badly
wounded and captured during the battle,
was to be ransomed but, when Henry IV
forbade this, he joined with his captors
and the following year fought alongside
Percy (on the losing side) against the King
at the Battle of Shrewsbury.

From the hamlet of Humbleton (limited
parking), set off up the lane opposite the
red telephone box signed for Humbleton

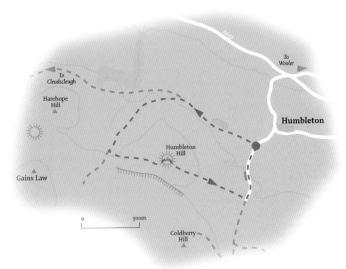

Burn. After passing some attractive cottages, go through the wooden gate by the blue public bridleway waymarker.

Turn right off the lane by the fingerpost to pick up the white hillfort trail waymarker. Go over the stile and continue on the grassy path, keeping to the white waymarkers past the pond, sweeping around the base of the rugged, rocky outcrops of Humbleton Hill.

Follow the grass path as it winds up to the left, staying on the left path at a fork.

Keep climbing gradually uphill on the path, through the purple heather, following the waymarkers to the summit.

As you come up onto the windswept top you can see the piles of old hillfort walls and a cairn which marks the summit. The hillfort was probably built around 300BC with walls two metres high and three metres thick, making it the most strongly defended fort on the fringes of the Cheviot Hills. Now there is just the pleasant quiet solitude of the grassy banks and the odd sheep bleating.

From the cairn, drop away between the piles of old stones marking an entrance to your right, and follow the distinct grass path heading southeast down through the bracken towards the town of Wooler.

The path leads steadily downhill off Humbleton; follow the white arrow across the field at the bottom towards the wooden five-bar gate and the lane back to Humbleton.

◄ The top of Humbleton Hill

Holy Island

Distance 5km **Time** 2 hours
Terrain pavements, tarmac
roads, grass tracks and rocky coastline
unsuitable for buggies **Map** OS Explorer
340 **Access** there is a bus service (477)
from Berwick-upon-Tweed which varies
in its frequency according to the tides

Joined to the mainland by a causeway
which can be crossed twice a day at
low tide, Lindisfarne – or Holy Island – is
a wonderful place to explore. This
straightforward walk visits the main
sights and a nature reserve.

The ruins of Lindisfarne Priory stand on
the site of a monastery founded by Saint
Aidan, an Irish monk who brought
Christianity to the Kingdom of
Northumbria in AD 635. His notable fifth
successor, Saint Cuthbert, is the patron
Saint of Northumberland. He lived as a
hermit on Inner Farne and the eider ducks
that live there are known as Cuddy Ducks
after him. A monk called Eadfrith
produced the internationally-important
Gospels on Lindisfarne in honour of
Cuthbert in around AD 721.

Set out from the main car park on the
island and make your way into the
picturesque fishing village of red-tiled
roofs, stone buildings, smart shops and
traditional pubs. After exploring the ruins
of the Priory carry on to the harbour
where you might catch sight of crab
fishermen at work by the upturned
cobble boats.

Walk by the pretty stone-shingled inlet
as the road follows the coastline directly
to Lindisfarne Castle which is perched
high and dramatically on a whinstone hill
called Beblowe Crag. You can see the bulk
of Muckle Cheviot in the distance if you
look back to the mainland.

Pass through the stile and continue up
the cobbles with the stunning sight of the
castle before you. You can visit the
National Trust-owned castle or follow the
track to the right to carry on the walk.

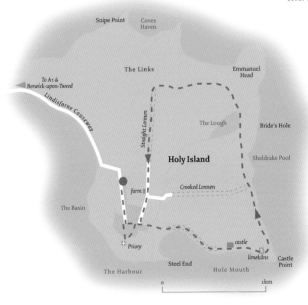

After exploring the limekilns behind the castle and Castle Point at the southeast tip of the island, turn left and follow the raised waggonway, built to transport limestone from the north of the island to the kilns for burning. Carry on, enjoying the birdlife and the view out to the Farne Islands.

Arriving at the pool and marsh of the Lough you can spend some time in the hide looking out for grebe, moorhen, coot and shoveler before continuing on the waggonway, crossing a stile on the way. At a kissing gate, turn left and follow the path by the farm wall, taking care not to disturb any of the rare breed sheep which graze here. Keep straight on until you reach the Straight Lonnen path which takes you through St Combs Farm and back to the car park and village.

Be sure to pick up a bottle of the famous Lindisfarne Mead – a potent aphrodisiac manufactured on the island – in one of the shops before heading home.

Please remember that there are safe crossing times to access and leave the island and you must pay attention to these. They are displayed by the roadside on the way on and off, and appear on the back page of the local weekly newspaper, *The Northumberland Gazette*. The tide will not wait for you!

◀ Lindisfarne Priory

Budle Bay

Distance **6.5km** Time **2 hours 30**
Terrain **roadside paths, beach and sand
dune paths** Map **OS Explorer 340**
Access **Arriva bus (501) from Berwick,
Morpeth, Alnwick and Newcastle**

**This circular route from the castle
at Bamburgh takes you along a
breathtaking beach and into Budle Bay
before returning through countryside.**

Bamburgh was the important ancient
capital of the Kingdom of Northumbria
and there have been fortifications on
top of the basalt outcrop for thousands
of years.

From the war memorial set in the rocky
base, head towards the cricket club
pavilion on the coast footpath. Bear right
on the path towards the stone walls, then
follow the path down towards the dunes
and beach. Turn left at the next blue
waymarker and follow the sand track as it
snakes through the ivy.

Follow the next waymarker up to the
right and continue on the track over the
dunes to the road. Keep on the roadside,
taking care of the traffic, as it swings
around giving great views of the beach,
before dropping down off the tarmac to
the lighthouse at Harkness Rocks, or Stag
Rocks, as they are also known, because of
the mysterious painting of a white stag
down by the shore.

Turn left up the grass track away from
the lighthouse and continue to bear
north on the worn trail. Keep on the
sandy trail, passing the last of the black
rocks as the view opens up on to the vast
expanse of golden sands which lead
around to Budle Bay.

Follow the beach around if the tide is out, exploring the high dunes at convenient points. There is also a higher path running by the side of the golf course if preferred. Make your way round past a crumbling old concrete pier and a small caravan park tucked in behind the dunes.

As the sea leads into Budle Bay, the sand gradually turns stonier; take the first stony track off the beach by the Lindisfarne Nature Reserve information board with life buoy.

Head straight up the stony track and through the wooden kissing gate by the cottages, before crossing the busy road, following the sign uphill for Waren.

Take care walking up the quiet roadside, past Budle Barn, and on uphill, passing the wooden fingerpost to Lonsdales Hill and the Coast Path sign on the left.

Turn left, following the Coast Path, over the break in the drystone wall and across the top of the crop field. Cross the stile and continue on the path by the hawthorn bushes and the rocky outcrop to a second stile. Cross and continue through the field by the waymarker, heading for the castle on the horizon; hug the contour of the hill by the gorse bushes and drop down to the wooden kissing gate.

Follow the path to the left on the farm access road, then turn right at the B1342, heading down the broad grass roadside path. Watch out for hares in the fields as you make your way past St Aidans Church back into town.

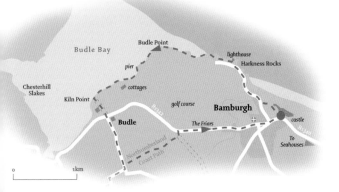

◄ Looking north over Budle Bay

Bamburgh circular

Distance 3.5km **Time** 1 hour 30
Terrain pavements, tarmac roads, sandy
beaches and sand tracks through dunes
with ascent that are unsuitable for
buggies **Map** OS Explorer 340
Access Arriva bus (501) from Berwick,
Morpeth, Alnwick and Newcastle

**Any trip to Bamburgh should include a
visit to the excellent Grace Darling
Museum and the Northumbrian
heroine's elaborate grave in the nearby
churchyard of St Aidans.**

The Longstone Lighthouse keeper's
daughter shot to national fame in 1838
when she rowed out with her father
William to rescue nine terrified survivors
of a shipwrecked paddlesteamer. Grace
held the small open cobble boat steady in
the roaring sea as her father helped the
survivors aboard. In all, 42 crew and
passengers of the *Forfarshire*, including the
captain and his wife, were lost.

Grace reluctantly became a popular
celebrity and was awarded the RNLI Medal
for Gallantry – the first woman to receive
the honour – but sadly died four years
later from tuberculosis aged just 27.

The museum on Radcliffe Road, with
the church directly opposite, is the
starting point for this circular walk that
takes in views of Bamburgh Castle, wide
golden beaches and the picturesque
village itself.

Set off down Church Street and turn left
down The Wynding, which is signed on
the facing stone wall of a house.

Take care of the traffic and follow the

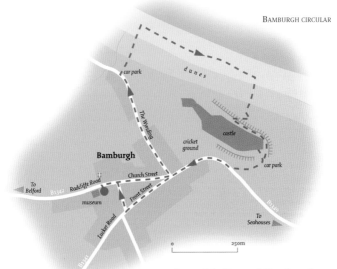

The following are labels on the map:

car park

d u n e s

The Wynding

Bamburgh

castle

cricket ground

car park

Church Street

To Belford

Radcliffe Road

B1342

Front Street

museum

Lucker Road

B1340

To Seahouses

B1341

0   250m

tarmac road down past the beautiful houses and into the second car park.

From here, you'll find easy access down onto the wide beach through rough high grasses on the dune tops by a line of old sunken anti-tank blocks.

Looking out to sea, you will see the Farne Islands on the horizon and the red-and-white painted Longstone Lighthouse.

There can be bracing winds whipping down the length of the vast beach so dress appropriately and set off south towards magnificent Bamburgh Castle.

Just before you draw level with the Windmill turret and St Oswald's Gate at the front of the castle walls, turn right and walk over the top of the rough grass dunes and onto a sandy path that runs through the shrubbery and skirts the volcanic whinstone outcrop that the

fortress is built upon. Follow the path around past the Battery Gate and up to the main entrance and gatehouse.

Owned by the Armstrong family (descendants of the Victorian industrialist Lord Armstrong who also built Cragside House near Rothbury), the castle is one of the most impressive in England and is well worth paying to visit. There are more than 2000 artefacts, including armour, arms, paintings and furniture, and 14 public rooms to explore, as well as an excellent café in the Clocktower.

From the castle go past the football and cricket pitches – with what must be the most dramatic sporting backdrop in the country – and follow the path back up the other side of the road from Church Street, past the triangle of trees in the centre of the village. Turn right to return to the Grace Darling Museum.

◀ Bamburgh Castle

Beadnell to Seahouses

Distance 4.5km **Time** 1 hour 45 (one way) **Terrain** pavement, dune paths and beach **Map** OS Explorer 340 **Access** buses from Craster, Embleton and Alnwick. Limited parking in Beadnell village

Spend time exploring some of the best rockpools on the coast on this easy walk from pretty Beadnell Harbour north to Seahouses.

The big walls of Beadnell Harbour protect only a handful of boats these days and the National Trust-owned limekilns, which would once have produced belching smoke, are long quietened. To start the walk follow the worn footpath around the side of the kilns and go along the grassy dune tops above the shoreline outcrops.

This path takes you to Ebb's Nook, site of a medieval chapel associated with St Aebba, a 7th-century Anglo-Saxon princess. There is little to see other than green humps, but recent excavations uncovered the bones of infants here; it is thought that this was an unconsecrated burial site for hundreds of years after the chapel went out of use.

Turn back at the far point of the Nook and retrace your steps to the information sign, turning right and dropping down onto the stony beach.

Head north until you see a wooden seat up on your left; leave the beach here and continue on Harbour Road. Follow the road around by the bay walls as Seahouses and the Farne Islands come into view. As you reach the last of the houses on

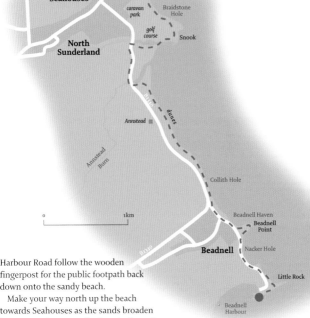

Seahouses

caravan park

Braidstone Hole

golf course

Snook

North Sunderland

Burn

dunes

Annstead

Annstead Burn

Collith Hole

0   1km

Beadnell Haven

Beadnell Point

B1340

Beadnell Nacker Hole

Little Rock

Beadnell Harbour

Harbour Road follow the wooden fingerpost for the public footpath back down onto the sandy beach.

Make your way north up the beach towards Seahouses as the sands broaden into a stunning unspoilt vista. At the end of the Annstead dunes, turn left off the beach and follow the track through the grass at the side of Annstead Burn heading west to a stone bridge. Turn onto the bridge and follow the path north past the golf course.

Pass the clubhouse and turn right at the public footpath sign, taking the path back down to the beach by the yellow waymarkers. Turn left just before you reach the end of North Sunderland Point,

following the yellow waymarker post through the golf course.

Continue on to a wooden kissing gate by the 14th tee box and go through, following the Coast Path sign for Seahouses along the clifftops.

Walk past the caravan park as the path turns right, down into North Sunderland harbour. Catch a boat out to the Farne Islands from here or turn around and make your way back to Beadnell.

◀ Beadnell Harbour   23

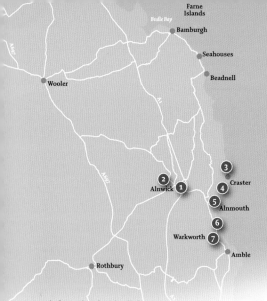

A certain boy wizard with a lightning flash scar on his forehead and glasses has worked his magic on Alnwick. Since appearing in the first *Harry Potter* movie as Hogwart School – it's in the scenes where the pupils are learning to fly their brooms – Alnwick Castle has become a mecca for fans of J K Rowling.

The Duchess of Northumberland has also worked her magic with the spellbinding Alnwick Gardens, making the ancient seat of the Percy family a fantastic place for a day out.

This chapter starts in Alnwick with a gentle tour of the countryside to the north of the castle, followed by an expedition in quiet estate grounds to visit the grand folly of Brizlee Tower.

Heading north up the coast to Craster,

don't forget to pick up some delicious kippers after your bracing walk out to the ruined but still mesmerising northern Camelot of Dunstanburgh. The little port is also the start point for an inland tour which returns by some unforgettable coastal views.

Where the River Aln runs into the North Sea at the elegant resort of Alnmouth is the next stop for two more enjoyable coastal strolls. The first walk visits a historic wartime defence on a tour of the town and the second takes you down the coast to the high walls of Warkworth Castle. The final walk visits a romantic beauty spot near the castle, accessed by rowing boat.

Sea air, stunning castles and fascinating history – now that's real magic.

Alnwick, Alnmouth and Warkworth

Tour of Alnwick

Distance 7km **Time** 2 hours
Terrain pavements, riverside and
woodland tracks **Map** OS Explorer 332
Access trains to Alnmouth from
Newcastle and Edinburgh with
connecting bus service. Arriva buses
(501,505, 518) from Newcastle
and Berwick

Once a major fortress on the Anglo-
Scottish border, the castle at Alnwick has
been the home of the distinguished
Percy family for over 700 years and
houses a stunning private art collection.
Adjacent to the castle, the Duchess of
Northumberland has created one of
Britain's most spectacular formal
gardens. This scenic riverside circular
walk takes you on a tour of Alnwick and
some of its surrounding countryside.

Start the walk from the Tenantry
Column, a monument erected in 1816 by
the townsfolk to thank the second Duke
of Northumberland for reducing their
rents. The straight-tailed lion on top is a
symbol of the Percy family.

Head past the war memorial on
Bondgate Without and on up past the old
railway station, now occupied by Barter
Books, Britain's biggest second-hand
bookstore, on the other side of the road.

Carry on to pass Bondgate Tower, a 15th-
century three-storey gatehouse, and make
your way up Bondgate Within and
Narrowgate to reach the front of
Alnwick Castle with its striking
battlement figures looking down.

Follow the road, known as the Peth, out
of town to soon reach the bridge over the
River Aln and another proud Percy lion.

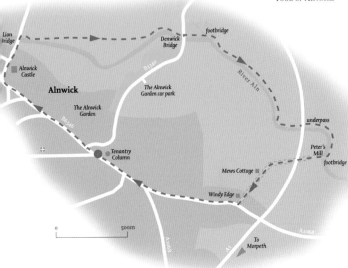

Just after the bridge, take the path on your right to cross the meadow on the northern bank of the river with views back over the water to the castle walls. Leaving the meadow, take care to cross the road over Denwick Bridge and follow the public footpath down to your right and into the woods.

Follow the worn dirt track through the undergrowth by the side of the river, then cross the bridge over the small burn and keep to the right-hand path as it rises up to meet a wooden kissing gate heading into a field.

Pass through and continue along the track by the river as it curves left and leads you to an underpass below the busy A1.

Continue on the path by the river and follow the waymarker to the right after you pass through a gate. This takes you along the course of the river, through another wooden gate which leads to the footbridge at Peter's Mill.

Cross the Aln and follow the farm track up to the next gate, then continue on the tarmac road through the underpass and on to the dead tree at the road.

Bear left up the tarmac country road, climbing uphill past a ruined farm building, to Mews Cottage. Head straight on to the roadside and turn right. Follow the pavements past Windy Edge Stables and on up by West Acres.

Stay on the pavement and follow the signs for the town centre back to the Tenantry Column – or Farmer's Folly, to give it its other name.

◄ Alnwick Castle's northern walls

Brizlee Tower

Distance 7km **Time** 2 hours
Terrain all-terrain buggy-friendly paths
and private roads, with a steep climb up
the road to the tower **Map** OS Explorer 332
Access trains to Alnmouth from
Newcastle and Edinburgh with
connecting bus service. Arriva buses
(501, 505, 518) from Newcastle and
Berwick. Hulne Park is only open between
11am and sunset; dogs, bikes and cars are
not allowed

**With its ever popular castle and gardens,
the town of Alnwick can get busy in the
tourist season – escape the crowds on
this walk to a secluded gothic tower
through the Duke of Northumberland's
Hulne Park.**

From the front of Alnwick Castle, head
left past the Bailiffgate Museum towards

the 15th-century St Michael's Church.

Cross the road at the church and head
uphill, past the Duchess's High School, on
the stone chippings path to the Hulne
Park Forest Lodge entrance.

The 3000-acre Hulne Park is the last
remaining of three parks that surrounded
Alnwick and provided the first medieval
Dukes of Northumberland with wood
and game. Famed landscape architect
Capabilty Brown worked with the 1st
Duke of Northumberland in the early
18th century to create much of the
parkland you see today.

Follow the private road with woods on
either side, safe in the knowledge that you
will only be passed by the occasional
estate vehicle or tractor. Keep an eye out
for red squirrels crossing on their high-
level rope bridge between the treetops.

◄ Brizlee Tower

Cross the stone bridge and continue on the Farm Drive, eventually coming to a yellow waymarker, which you follow, by the standing stone sign. (There is a longer red waymarked trail from here to the ruins of Hulne Abbey, if you would like to extend this walk.)

To reach Brizlee Tower, turn left at the next yellow waymarker up the steep White Hill, taking care not to disturb the grouse at the roadsides. Keep right at the top of the hill to reach the imposing tower in a clearing in the woods.

Built by the celebrated Scottish architect Robert Adam for Hugh Percy, the first Duke of Northumberland, to commemorate his wife, Lady Elizabeth Seymour, who died in 1776, the tower is an ornate 26-metre high Grade 1-listed building with commanding views over the surrounding countryside.

Above the balcony, under the Duke's crest, a Latin inscription translates as 'Look around! I have measured out all these things; they are my orders, it is my planning; many of these trees have even been planted by my hand'.

You can carry on from the tower to complete a short loop of the top of Brizlee Hill or head back the way you came, turning right at the bottom of the hill onto the private road and back through the park into Alnwick.

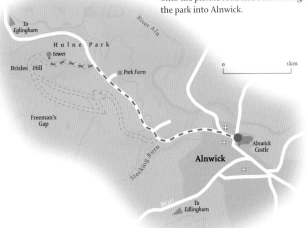

Dunstanburgh Castle

Distance 7km **Time** 2 hours **Terrain** grass tracks and farm tracks **Map** OS Explorer 332 **Access** car park just before village (£2 all day), Arriva bus (501) from Morpeth and Berwick. Entry fee for Dunstanburgh Castle, except for English Heritage members

Enjoy some wonderful coastal views on this circular walk which takes in the iconic fortress of Dunstanburgh Castle, before returning via farmland to the pretty harbour at Craster.

Park in the Quarry car park on the edge of Craster village. The very hard-wearing whinstone quarried here was shipped out from Craster harbour and used as cobbles and kerbstones all over England – 'whin' is the sound made when the rock is struck by a stonemason's hammer. Make your way down to the harbour and then go left along Dunstanburgh Road to the kissing gate and the start of a long easy stroll out to Dunstanburgh Castle.

This section of the walk is always popular, so if you want it to yourself, go very early in the morning.

The imposing castle draws you steadily on and after the little inlet of Nova Scotia, a long incline brings you to the gatehouse entrance. Now managed by English Heritage, the building of the massive headland fortress was begun by the ambitious Earl Thomas of Lancaster in 1313. He saw the grand project as a second Camelot; unfortunately, he also saw

himself as a second Arthur and was not long afterwards executed for treason by Edward II, never having seen his project completed.

Ownership eventually passed into the hands of John of Gaunt who, in his role as Lieutenant of the Scottish Marches, strengthened it against attacks from ever-marauding Scots. The War of the Roses, when the castle became a Lancastrian stronghold, saw the castle besieged several times and newly-developed artillery left Dunstanburgh a shattered ruin. It is a tribute to the original builders that there is so much of it still standing.

Bear left before the entrance and carry on round, picking up the coast path above the rocky shore. The north walls of the castle sit on Gull Crag and in summer countless kittiwakes nest in the cliff.

Pass by the golf course and a pillbox before dropping down to the sands of Embleton Bay. You can easily extend this walk by continuing north on the beach to Low Newton and the lovely secluded bay of Football Hole just beyond.

After enjoying the beach, head inland by the path just after the second pillbox and follow the road to the farm. Turn left to pass the holiday cottages and, when the driveway curves right, carry on to a gate which takes you out onto farmland. Carry on along the track, past an old limekiln and between a pair of pillboxes to

eventually come to the farm at Dunstan Square. Go through the gate and turn left, following the wide grassy path signposted for Craster and Dunstanburgh Castle.

Head towards the gap known as the Shaird by Scrog Hill and, after going through a gate, turn right to follow the path along the base of the gorse-covered whinstone cliffs, or 'heughs' as they are known locally. This rough path takes you back to the road into Craster where the best kippers in the country await.

◄ Approaching Dunstanburgh

Craster and Howick

Distance 10km **Time** 2 hours
Terrain grass tracks, pavements, chipping
paths and coastal trails **Map** OS Explorer
332 **Access** car park just before village
(£2 all day), Arriva bus (501) from Morpeth
and Berwick

People have been living on the
Northumberland coastline for centuries
and this pleasant circular walk from the
pretty fishing village of Craster takes
you past an important Mesolithic site
at Howick.

Park in the Quarry car park on the edge
of Craster village – the visitor information
centre here has panels detailing life in the
Middle Stone Age Period. Enter the Arnold

Memorial Northumberland Wildlife Trust
Reserve and follow the signposted path to
Craster South Farm. Go through the
wooden gate, following the yellow
waymarker, and across the pasture field
on the path to a gate by the road.

Bear left as you cross over the road, then
head up the track towards the cottages,
following the track as it continues along
the field edge. At the kissing gate, take the
signed path for Howick Hall and go past
the rocky escarpment of Hips Heugh. Pass
through the next kissing gate and
continue on the track by the top of the
field by the woods.

Keep going along the field edge until you
reach a broad twin tyre track leading off to

your right through the woods. Follow this track up to the roadside entrance to Howick Hall, the ancestral seat of the Earls Grey.

Prime Minister Charles Grey, 2nd Earl Grey, gave his name to the famous tea after a blend with bergamot extract – which gives the brew its distinctive aroma – was created for him by a Chinese mandarin to offset the lime found in the local Howick water. The formal gardens at the hall are open to the public from early February until mid Novermber.

At the road, turn left and head east on the narrow roadside path through the trees. Take care at the Howick junction and continue gradually uphill until you reach the farm road for Sea Houses.

Follow the wooden footpath sign through the kissing gate and head down towards the sea. A chance discovery of pieces of flint in a cliff edge here by two amateur archaeologists led to excavations in 2000 and 2002 by Newcastle University which unearthed over 18,000 pieces of flint and many other significant items. Red ochre pieces were also found at the site, which led the experts to believe that the ancient people of Howick may have painted their bodies. (The university have constructed a Mesolithic roundhouse from their findings which you can see at

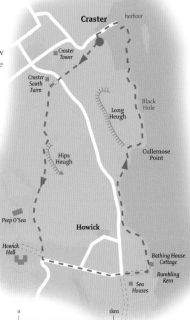

Maelmin, 8km north of Wooler).

Turn left through the next gate, heading past the hardy 18th-century Bathing House cottage, and follow the well-surfaced coast path by the spectacular rocky sea edge and around Cullernose Point back into Craster.

From the pub beer garden, with Robson's famous kipper smokehouse opposite, head right down to the harbour before taking the road past the Lifeboat Station back to the car park.

◾ Bathing House cottage

33

Around Alnmouth

**Distance 7km Time 2 hours
Terrain** pavements, beach, grass and dirt
tracks **Map** OS Explorer 332 **Access** trains
from Newcastle and Edinburgh or Arriva
bus (518) from Morpeth and Alnwick

**The beach at Alnmouth was a favourite
spot for Victorian Tynesiders who came
here to enjoy the sea air and holiday in
the town's elegant hotels. This looped
walk takes in the expansive beach after a
stroll through town and returns via an
interesting wartime relic and museum.**

Start from the train station at Hipsburn
(there is also parking beside the beach at
Alnmouth Common midway on the walk).
Turn left at the bus stop and head east
down South View Road to the
roundabout. Take care crossing the B1338
and follow the sign for Alnmouth, past
fields on your right and Hipsburn First
School on your left.

Continue over the footbridge and up
the hill to cross the road at the war
memorial. Turn right into Alnmouth at
Northumberland Street and take the first
left at The Wynd, following Marine Road,
all the way down to the car park on the
beach at the golf club.

Head north up the unspoilt sandy
beach towards Seaton Point, enjoying the
glorious view out over the North Sea.

After the sand turns to rock, leave the
beach at Foxton Hall golf club and go over
the pebbles and through the kissing gate
signed for the Coast Path. Head up the
concrete path to the golf club and turn
left to follow the waymarked trail past
the 18th hole. Cross the fairway, being
respectful of golfers, and continue over
the top of the grassy dunes heading
back south.

Keep to the path on the right, past the
caravans, and follow the trail up the side

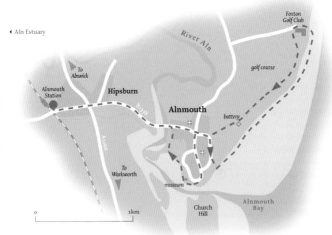

◀ Aln Estuary

River Aln

Foxton
Golf Club

*To
Alnwick*

Alnmouth
Station

Hipsburn

golf course

Alnmouth

battery

*To
Warkworth*

museum

Alnmouth
Bay

Church
Hill

0   1km

of the rough grass by the wall.

Off to the left of the path is Alnmouth Battery; a stone and brick-built Grade II-listed building built in 1881 by the Duke of Northumberland for use by the Percy Artillery Volunteers to protect against French invaders. It was later made into a pillbox during the Second World War.

It's not safe to go inside the battery so carry on past the benches and flame signal. Drop down the track through the trees to rejoin the road at The Wynd and carry on along Northumberland Street, past the shops and the Hope and Anchor and Schooner hotels.

Following Riverside Road around, you will see Church Hill on the far bank of the estuary. Alnmouth was once an important grain-importing port, but when the course of the river was swept away from the harbour during a violent storm in 1806

the hill – site of Saxon church ruins – became stranded from the rest of the village. The last of the church was also lost in the storm; the prominent wooden cross marks where it stood.

Look out also for a small black fisherman's hut next to the upturned boats on your right as you head inland. This is one of the smallest museums in the country and contains interesting local memorabilia and old photographs of fishermen and the ferrymen who once took passengers across the estuary from here.

Continue on Riverside Road, then take a sharp left to follow the narrow Lover's Walk which runs alongside the children's playpark. This takes you back to the Duchess Bridge where you turn left to return to the start.

Alnmouth to Warkworth

Distance 8km Time **3 hours**
Terrain **pavements, compacted tracks,
dirt tracks and sand** Map **OS Explorer 332
Access trains to Alnmouth from
Newcastle and Edinburgh. Arriva bus
(518) from Morpeth and Alnwick**

**Take a hike between two of the
county's most picturesque villages on
a stunning section of the 103km-long
Northumberland Coast Path.**

From the bus stop at the Parish Church
of St John the Baptist, in the centre of
Alnmouth, head south down past the
Schooner Hotel to Riverside Road,
following the blue Coast Path waymarker.

Keep on the pavement as it swings right
by the boats on the Aln Estuary and carries
on past the children's playpark. Turn
sharply left onto Lovers' Walk and follow

the narrow lane around past the fields and
on to Duchess Bridge. The huge white golf
ball on the horizon is the radar station at
RAF Boulmer.

Go up the steps and through the white
gate, then cross the road and turn left
towards Hipsburn. Keep on the pavement
as you approach Alnmouth and Lesbury
Cricket Club, then cross the road and head
left following the wooden signposts.

There can be hundreds of chattering
sparrows in the hawthorns alongside the
track here. Go over the wooden bridge,
following the black metal sign for
Warkworth. Do not go through the kissing
gate onto the saltmarsh but follow the
path uphill to the right. Turn left at the
wooden memorial seat and continue on
the path behind the hedgerow heading
south. After a mile or so the trail crosses a

◂ Warkworth Castle

road; follow the wooden Warkworth signpost. You will see the lighthouse on Coquet Island to the southeast as you continue to head towards medieval Warkworth.

Turn left at the next signpost for the Public Bridleway to Buston Links and go down towards the sea. At the bottom of the hill follow the sign for Birling Carrs through the bracken and along the back of the dunes.

Climb steadily uphill for spectacular views of the beach and sea and keep on the track alongside the wall as it drops down to the caravan park. Cross the small wooden bridge and, if the sea is out, turn left onto the beach and explore the rocky wave-washed outcrop of Birling Carrs. (If the sea is in, continue on the bridlepath and coast route through the caravan park and across the back of the dunes.)

Turn right on the golden sands and continue south towards Coquet Island, over the rocks and past the long line of concrete anti-tank blocks. Go on down the beach for a while before turning right at the wide path by two more half-sunken anti-tank blocks and a life buoy.

Head up the signed tarmac path to a car park with a toilet block. From here head

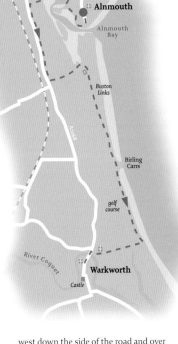

west down the side of the road and over the bridge into beautiful Warkworth, which sits above the River Coquet. Spend some time exploring the castle before catching a bus back to Alnmouth.

Warkworth Castle and the Hermitage

Distance 2km **Time** 1 hour (allow more
time to explore the Hermitage)
Terrain all-terrain buggy-friendly,
compact tracks with steep ascents and
descents **Map** OS Explorer 332
Access Arriva bus (518) from Alnwick
and Morpeth. Car parking at Warkworth
Castle (parking charge refunded if you
visit castle)

Warkworth's impressive sandstone castle
overlooks the pretty village from a
hilltop on a loop of the River Coquet.
There has been a castle here since the
Norman Conquest, but it is most closely
associated with the Dukes of
Northumberland who restored and
strengthened it in the late 19th-century.

Start the walk in the castle car park and
follow the path signed for the Hermitage
down the leafy bank towards the broad
River Coquet.

Go steeply downhill and follow the
riverbank under the trees and on past a
mooring, where you can hire boats to row
up the river. Continue on the Mill Walk,
go through the kissing gate and follow
the path on over the field until you see
the Hermitage cut into the red rock crag
on the opposite bank. On Wednesdays,
Sundays and bank holidays during the
summer months you can summon the
ferryman here to take you across to the
Hermitage by ringing the bell (check at
castle beforehand).

The Hermitage, a two-storey structure
dating from the late 14th century, consists
of two parts, an outer stone-built section

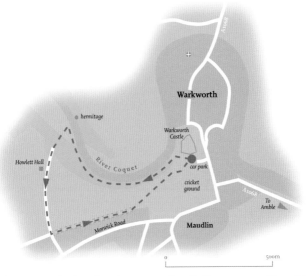

and an inner portion hewn from the sandstone and made into a chapel, with rib vaulting and an alter, a sacristy and two smaller chambers. Look out for an interesting, but hard to spot, nativity scene carving.

A Latin inscription carved into the stone above the door to the cave is from Psalm 42.3 and reads 'My tears have been my meat day and night'. This chimes with the fanciful tale that the chapel was built by Sir Bertram of Bothal, an unfortunate knight who mistakenly killed his own brother as well as his lover, one Isabel Widdrington, whilst trying to rescue the latter from a band of Scottish Reivers. He was said to have spent the rest of his life in grief at the Hermitage.

In truth, there were several 'hermits' employed by the Earls of Northumberland until the Dissolution of the Monasteries in the 16th century. It was a pretty good job; in return for saying prayers for the Earl, the hermit had pasture for his cows, firewood, a garden, fish on Sundays and a small salary. As the Hermitage was also a popular place of pilgrimage, he would probably have benefited from generous alms-giving too.

From the ferry landing, turn up the public footpath, past Howlett Hall and onto the road. Just before you reach the smart houses at the top of the bank, turn left and follow the lane along the edge of the field. This leads to a path which cuts across a field to the village cricket ground.

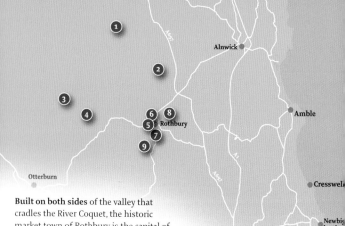

Built on both sides of the valley that cradles the River Coquet, the historic market town of Rothbury is the capital of Coquetdale and the gateway to a magnificent area of rolling hills, gurgling burns and pretty villages such as Hepple, Holystone and Harbottle.

This section begins further north, however, in the much less populated Breamish Valley. Rich in archaeological interest, the Hillfort Trail is a great introduction to an area that is sure to call you back. Further down the A697, the next walk detours off for a short forestry tour with great views in Thrunton Woods.

Deep into Coquetdale, by Harbottle, the walk up to the enigmatic Drake Stone shows off all that is special about this landscape. You can't fail also to be enchanted by the short stroll to the Lady's Well by Holystone; scores of pilgrims once made their way from all over Northumberland to this beautiful spot.

Three walks of different character start from Rothbury. The first route takes you along the Coquet and through farmland to the nearby village of Thropton for a return by local bus. The second is a more demanding tour of the hillside to the north of the market town which follows the Carriage Drive, thoughtfully provided by Victorian industrialist Lord Armstrong of Cragside. The final walk from the town follows some of the course of the railway that once served the town.

Not far east of Rothbury, Lord Armstrong's playground at National Trust-owned Cragside is the setting for an entertaining ramble through his huge and imaginatively landscaped gardens. Highlights include lakes, dragonflies, rhododendrons, red squirrels and towering trees. The final walk takes you up into the wilds of Simonside to discover a bandits' hideout and returns by Dove Crag, a great spot from which to survey the valley below.

Breamish, Coquetdale and Rothbury

Breamish Hillfort Trail

Distance **4.5km** Time **2 hours**
Terrain **grass tracks with waymarkers and
some steep ascent** Map **OS Explorer OL16**
Access **free parking at Bulby's Wood, west
of Ingram, near Powburn off the A697. No
public transport to Ingram**

**A circular walk above the River Breamish,
beginning with a stiff climb, which takes
in the sites of three ancient hillforts.**

Start from Bulby's Wood car park (with
toilets) on the south bank of the River
Breamish, just under 1km west of Ingram
National Park Centre.

Cross the road and follow the white
Hillfort Trail waymarker up the steep
grass track and through the bracken, then
turn to the right at the next waymarker as
the path goes on uphill.

Continue to ascend, enjoying the views

back over the Breamish, following the
white waymarkers and making towards
the edge of the wood.

The path gets gradually steeper and
it takes a bit of a pull up to the plateau
for spectacular views back down the
valley. The remains of a Roman-period
farmstead can be seen towards the crest
of the hill here. Take the path past the
edge of the plantation and on to the top
of Brough Law and the impressive Iron
Age hillfort, with its double ring of fallen
defensive walls.

After exploring the fort, come back
out of the entrance and turn right,
following the grass track to the next white
waymarker and continue on over the
windswept upland heath, heading
towards the high point of Ewe Hill.

Stay on the grass track until you reach

◀ The River Breamish

the next waymarker post and take the trail to the left heading for the cultivation terraces and fort at Turf Knowe. (You can extend your walk here by following the waymarker to explore the hillfort and a hidden ravine at Middle Dean.)

The second fort at Turf Knowe is unusual in that it has three walls made up of different coloured rocks. Two Bronze Age burial cairns have also been discovered here; evidence that this place was used as a burial or ritual site over 2000 years ago.

From here it is an easy descent back down into the valley on the wide grassy path to visit the third hillfort of the day. The fort on Ingram Hill is the lowest-lying ancient settlement in the Breamish Valley and was also occupied during the Roman period.

The track continues downhill through the bracken to the roadside, where you turn left for the riverside car park. You should take time to explore the glittering waters of the Breamish from the shingle banks before setting off home.

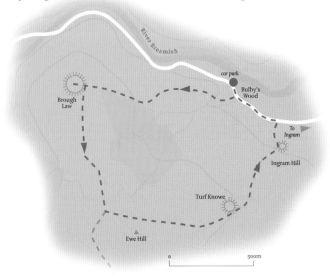

Thrunton Woods

Distance 3km **Time** 1 hour
Terrain woodland tracks and paths with
some steep ascent **Map** OS Explorer 332
Access car park (free) at Thrunton Woods,
signposted off the A697 just past the
Moor House Crossroads

**This family-friendly walk is the easiest
of three waymarked trails in the Forestry
Commission-managed Thrunton Woods.**

The woods here are planted on and
around two steep sandstone escarpments
– Thrunton Crag in the north and Long
Crag/Coe Crag to the south – which
provide great viewpoints over the
Northumbrian countryside.

The crags also have a history as handy
hideouts for local hoodlums; a robber
called Thomas Wedderburn was on the
run from the law in the wilds of the
Alnwick Moors and hid in a cave on the
north ridge of crags where Thrunton
Woods now stand. Unfortunately for
Thomas, he was smoked out with oil
lamps and gunned down with musket
shot. The woods also contain McCartney's
Cave, a spot reputed to have been hand-
carved out of the rock by a monk, but also
used by desperadoes looking to avoid the
tough justice meted out by those in
power during the county's violent past.

From the information board in the
car park, follow the green arrow
waymarkers for the Green Crag Top Trail
uphill into the woods. The gradient rises
steadily as the track bears right at the
brow of the hill.

Stay on the trail as it levels out, taking
you through the bracken and pleasant
coniferous woodland. Roe deer, badgers

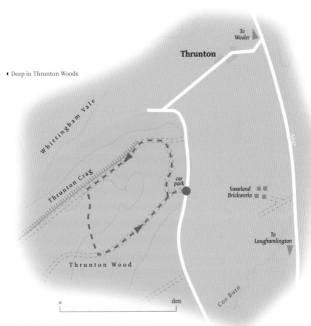

◀ Deep in Thrunton Woods

and red squirrels are among the wildlife that can all be seen in the woods. Look out, too, for mountain bikers; Thrunton is full of well-hidden rooty singletrack routes through the trees and riders use the wide forestry tracks to access them.

The trail drops down and swings left before climbing steeply back uphill. As the trail levels off again, keep following the regular waymarkers to a seat with spectacular views over Whittingham Vale.

Turn left to continue on a woodland track past rhododendron bushes to a huge boulder left behind after the last ice age.

Keep going uphill, then turn left at the next wooden seat and drop down again on the broad path. As the trail levels off follow the green waymarker down to the access road that leads you all the way back down to the car park.

The Drake Stone

Distance 4km **Time** 2 hours
Terrain steep ascents, chipping forest
tracks, grass tracks, worn trails, wet and
boggy land, roadside walking
Map OS Explorer 0L16 **Access** no public
transport to Harbottle. Car park (free) at
West Woods

This circular hill walk in the Coquet
Valley takes in the Drake Stone, a free
standing 30-foot-high block of sandstone
said to have magical properties.

Set off from the car park on the left after
going through Harbottle and follow the
signpost up the red chipping forest track.
It's a steep climb through the trees, but
you are soon out on open bracken-
covered hillside. Carry on to reach a seat
with views back down the valley.

This land backs onto MOD ranges; if the
red flag is flying then live firing is taking
place. Don't pick up any metal objects
which may be lying around.

Keep on the worn track up past a cairn
to reach boulders and scree and then the
impressive Drake Stone itself. Thought to
have magical healing properties, the huge
boulder is said to have been sacred to
ancient druids who healed sickly children
by passing them around it. More recently,
workmen were frightened off from an
attempt to drain the lake above when a
disembodied voice is said to have
emanated from the stone, saying: 'Let
alone, let alone, or I'll droon Harbottle
and the Peels and bonny Holystone'.

Turn right on the small track through
the limestone boulders and continue

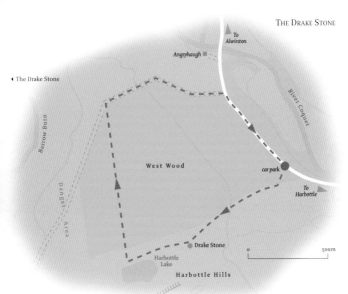

To Alwinton

Angryhaugh

◄ The Drake Stone

River Coquet

Barrow Burn

Danger Area

West Wood

car park

To Harbottle

Drake Stone

Harbottle Lake

Harbottle Hills

0   500m

down the track to your left, through the heather to the black glacial pool of Harbottle Lake.

Follow the yellow footpath marker over the wooden stile and around the north edge of the water, where things can get very boggy. Go on until you reach the fence by the MOD sign and turn right, heading north by the fence uphill along the stony track that leads you into the woods at the top.

Go straight ahead into the forest, following the line of old concrete fenceposts, and keep heading north. The track is boggy in places, but keep with it until you reach a wooden kissing gate.

Turn right over the cattle grid out of the wood and continue along the grassy chippings track by the wall as it swings

downhill towards St Michael's Church.

The village of Alwinton sits below you to the left and if you continue on up into the rolling green hills of the Upper Coquet Valley you'll be in the centre of Northumberland's old illicit whisky trade. Stills were hidden in the heather and plenty of duty-free bottles made their way into the fantastically-named Slyme Foot pub, which is sadly long gone.

Go over the second cattle grid and keep on the track down to the road. Pass through the five-bar gate and turn right, taking care along the roadside as you return to the car park.

Before leaving Harbottle it is worth exploring the ruins of the medieval castle which sits on a mound to the west of the quiet village.

The Lady's Well

Distance 1km **Time** 45 minutes
Terrain woodland tracks, grass tracks and
roadside **Map** OS Explorer OL42 **Access** no
public transport to Holystone. Forestry
Commission car park at Holystone

**All the family can enjoy this short
woodland and field trail to an
atmospheric well where 3000 pagan
Northumbrian are said to have been
baptised in AD627.**

This easy circular route is an excellent
walk for small children, although a
narrow kissing gate as you exit the woods
makes it unsuitable for buggies.

Go through the village of Holystone,
following the sign for woodland walks,
and park in the Forestry Commission
car park. From the information board,
take the green waymarked trail

on the path to the right through the
spruce forest.

Turn right into the woods at the
green sign for the Lady's Well and
continue through the pine needles
and rutted tree roots.

Come out of the forest at the narrow
wooden kissing gate and head straight
across the field towards the small
woodland enclosure directly in front of
you. Skirt around the edge of the wall to
find the entrance to the Lady's Well.

A stone Celtic cross stands in the
middle of the water and a statue of St
Paulinus, who baptised all those
Northumbrians here during Easter week,
stands opposite. The early kings of
Northumbria were pagans until King
Edwin converted to Christianity when he
married Ethelberga, a princess from Kent.

◀ The Lady's Well

Paulinus was her chaplain and had come to Kent from Rome under the orders of Pope Gregory. Following King Edwin's death in battle, most Northumbrians slowly reverted back to paganism until King Oswald brought south the Irish missionary Aidan from St Columba's monastery on Iona and granted him the island of Lindisfarne as the site for the first Christian monastery in Northumbria.

The well was at one time a watering place, or more likely a shrine, beside the Roman road running from Bremenium in Redesdale all the way out to the coast. It is also associated with St Ninian, the Bishop of Whithorn, in south-west Scotland, who is said to have visited in the 6th century. The site is thought to

have gained its name from nuns belonging to the Augustinian convent at Holystone.

Come back out by the five-bar gate and follow the public footpath sign straight down the field to a second gate at the bottom.

Go through and turn immediately right, going through the two wooden gates on a grass track between the house and the old railway stock carriage, following the waymarked public footpath.

Continue over the field diagonally to your left across the marshy land, heading for the wooden stile. Cross over the fence and go onto the road, taking care as you head to your right, back up to the car park where you set off from.

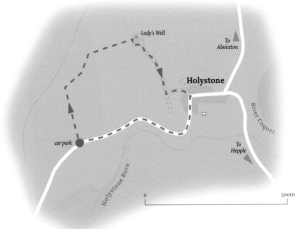

Rothbury to Thropton

Distance 5.6km (one way) **Time** 1 hour 30
Terrain pebbled paths, dirt tracks,
roadside and pavement
Map OS Landranger 81 **Access Arriva bus**
(144) from Morpeth (no Sunday service);
return to Rothbury by bus

This walk follows the Coquet upstream
from Rothbury to Thropton; keep your
eyes peeled for the blue flash of a
majestic kingfisher as these beautiful
little birds inhabit the banks along the
first part of this route.

Starting from the Cowhaugh car park by
the metal bridge in Rothbury (pay and
display), cross over to the children's
playpark and follow the riverside track up
to the left.

Keep on the path through the bushes at
the river edge and enjoy the spectacular
views of the Simonside Ridge on the
other side of the river.

Continue past the golf course bridge
and follow the path up by the hawthorn
bushes. Go through the wooden gates and
on down the bank bearing left to the
metal Lady's Bridge.

Rothbury's golf course stands on the
fields where the town's popular horse
races were held annually from 1759 until
the last meeting in 1965. Looking back up
to your right across the water you will see
the gorse bushes on the slopes of
Gallowfield Brae where Coquetdale's
criminals once met their grim end.

Should you fancy seeing what the
gallows looked like then you can pay a
macabre visit to a gibbet, complete with

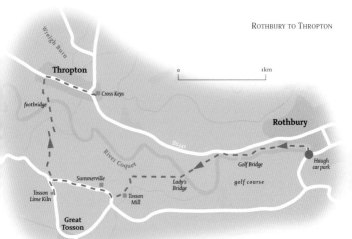

hanging wooden head, on the hill above the village of Elsdon 19km west in the neighbouring valley of Redesdale, where a criminal named William Winter was strung up in 1792 following his execution at Westgate in Newcastle-upon-Tyne.

From the Lady's Bridge, head west away from the river on the grass track by the farmer's fence and hawthorn hedges until you reach the tarmac road at Tosson Mill.

Carry on up the hill past the World War Two pillbox and turn right down the road signposted for Bickerton. Go on past Summerville House and continue on the roadside until you reach the wooden sign for Thropton. Before following this sign through the fields, however, it is worthwhile detouring left along the road towards Great Tosson to visit the solidly-built Tosson Lime Kiln; probably the best preserved example of a rural kiln in Northumberland.

Returning to the junction, follow the marked route across the fields and through three gates before arriving at the river and a metal footbridge.

Cross it and follow the narrow path to your left, then turn first right up past the houses on the tarmac road and up into the village of Thropton. Turn right again at the top of the lane by the village hall and make your way down past the picturesque stone cottages.

Cross the footbridge next to the stone roadbridge over the Wreigh Burn and head up the hill to the Cross Keys pub. Enjoy a pint while you're waiting for the next bus back to Rothbury to arrive.

Be warned, however, that whisky may not be the only spirit in the small ivy-covered hostelry. A former landlord was spooked enough to go to the press in 1988 after experiencing a series of ghostly events including phantom footsteps and unexplained bangs in the cellar.

◀ The Lady's Bridge over the River Coquet

The Carriage Drive

Distance 12km **Time** 4 hours
Terrain field paths, compacted tracks, road
Map OS Landranger 81 **Access** Arriva bus
(144) from Morpeth (no Sunday service)

**Your efforts are rewarded with stunning
views of Rothbury on this circular walk
which winds its way around the hills
above the market town.**

From Rothbury's war memorial, head
up the narrow alley beside the Co-op. Turn
left at the top, then take the first right up
the next narrow path (signposted for
Hillside Road) that leads up past the
cottages of Backcrofts.

Turn right at the top onto Hillside East
and follow the road past the houses and
the trees to a wooden gate up on your left.
Take the path up the steep grassy field,
passing Addycombe Farm on your right as
you rise steadily, enjoying the views back
down over Rothbury.

When you reach the kissing gate at the
top of the field, turn left onto the Carriage
Drive, created by Lord Armstrong of nearby
Cragside for the enjoyment of his house
guests. Follow the drive on through the
woodland with rhododendron and scrub
packed with bilberries. Take the right-hand
path uphill at the fork and continue
until you eventually come to a five-bar
gate and stile that exits the forest. Stay
with the drive as you cross the moorland;
look out for basking adders in the
summer. Ahead of you, the taller of the
two huge boulders left by the receding ice
cap is Ship Crag.

Keep on the drive past the television
mast, then follow the worn sheep tracks to
your left to reach the cairn for a superb
view over Rothbury. Return to the drive
and continue to head west, on past a trig
point up on the hillside to your right.

After following the drive around the

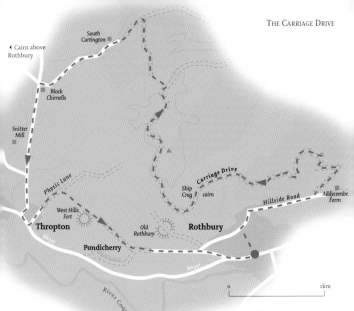

hillside, leave the red chippings track at a yellow waymarker for open heather moorland. Cross the Open Access Land and go over the stone steps, heading down the rutted track by the drystone wall to the next waymarker. Turn left into the woods and drop down through the forest, then turn left again at the Forest Enterprise Blue Mill sign.

Head down the quiet road and continue to Black Chirnells Cottage, where you turn left for Thropton, taking care on the roadside. Just past the Cross Keys, turn left onto the leafy lane of Physic Lonnen.

The Knights Hospitallers of St John of Jerusalem had a hospital here in the 13th and 14th centuries and there is a spring on your right about halfway up, opposite Physic Cottage. Carry on up to the blue waymarked gate and follow the grass track to the wooden stile.

Turn right, and head up the field to the stone steps in the wall which lead you to the Iron Age West Hills camp and a nearby 3500 year old burial cairn.

Go through the wooden gate and follow the yellow waymarkers down the track to the road. Walk past the houses along Pondicherry all the way along to the top of Gravelly Bank – the field to your right is known as Beggars Rigg. Continue until you see the former County Hotel building then follow the pavement back down to the war memorial.

The Old Railway Line

Distance 3.2km **Time** 1 hour 15
Terrain roads, pavements, dirt tracks
with a loose gravel ascent to Garleigh
Bank **Map** OS Landranger 81
Access Arriva bus (14) from Morpeth
(no Sunday service)

Doctor Beeching's axe fell on the
Rothbury Branch railway line in 1963.
The line had already been closed to
passengers nine years earlier and no sign
of the smart brick and wood station
house and platform is left. The pleasant
track, which once wound its way through
the green countryside to Scot's Gap and
on to Morpeth, now provides the basis
for an agreeable circular hike.

Set out from the main car park at the
Cowhaugh in Rothbury (pay and display).
Follow the footpath east alongside the
river and past the spring which flows into
the Coquet at Donkin's Well and the main
stone bridge in town.

Continue past the smart houses of
Station Road until you come to the
entrance of the industrial estate by the
metal pens of the auction market. This is
where the line ended in three sidings
and a platform; the large Coquet
Vale Hotel (formerly the Station Hotel)
to your right was built to accommodate
railway passengers. The line was originally
intended to go on through the
countryside and over the border to
Kelso, but it was never built.

Continue on the road through the
industrial estate until you reach a
builders' yard at the bottom. Bear left and
follow the dirt track into the wooded area
and continue up the track to where you

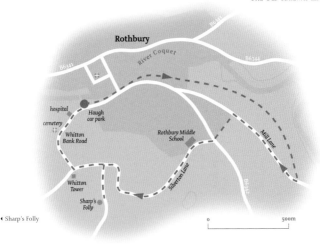

◀ Sharp's Folly

are met by the imposing overgrown high rockfaces either side of you that were blasted through to lay the railway tracks. A derelict and unsafe wooden footbridge spans the gap further on. Go east along the well-worn country path until you reach the tarmac road heading down to Wagtail Farm.

The old railway line carries on past the farm, but turn right back towards Rothbury onto Mill Lane, which runs to Wagtail Lane, and then left up the gravel track when you reach the houses. It's a steady climb past the front of the houses of Lordenshaws Drive to the top of Garleigh Bank where you cross the road and go straight on past Rothbury Middle School on your right.

The meadowland sweeps down from the crags of Simonside as you follow Silverton Lane on past Whitton Farm.

Take a small detour up the Hillhead Road to your left as you pass the farm buildings, signed for Whitton Hillhead, and visit Sharp's Folly, a listed circular stone-built tower which the Rev. Dr Thomas Sharp had erected to relieve unemployment among local stonemasons in the 18th century. The good reverend also had an interest in astronomy and it's thought that he used it as an observatory. The building is in a dangerous condition inside and cannot be entered.

Return to Carterside Road and continue until you reach the spring that pours out of the wall at Whitton Tower, a former pele, then rectory, and head right down the bank on Whitton Bank Road that passes the cemetery and Coquetdale Cottage Hospital. The path leads you straight back to the car park at the bottom of the hill.

Lakes of Cragside

Distance 4km **Time** 2 hours
Terrain forest and lakeside paths and
trails, some stone steps and tree-rutted
tracks. Not suitable for buggies, although
plenty of paths around the grounds are
Map OS Landranger 81 **Access** Arriva bus
(144) to Rothbury from Morpeth. Arriva
bus (508) from Gateshead Metro Centre
to Cragside Sundays and Bank Holidays
in the summer (May to October).
National Trust admission prices apply

**Walk around the spectacular grounds of
a Victorian industrialist's singular home
and see towering trees, one of Europe's
largest rock gardens and pretty
dragonflies by tranquil lake sides.**

Lord Armstrong's Cragside home was
the first in the world to be lit by hydro-
electricity and is crammed with gadgets
and paintings. The son of a Newcastle
corn merchant, William George
Armstrong was a solicitor-turned-
engineer who made his fortune from

armaments during the Crimean conflict,
supplied weapons to both the Unionists
and Confederates in the American Civil
War and founded a sprawling shipyard
and factory at Elswick on the Tyne which
employed thousands of men.

From the visitor centre, go right into the
main car park and continue on the upper
level, heading past the information hut
towards the house.

Turn left uphill into the trees, following
the Slipper Lake fingerpost, and continue
up the gravel track above the house by the
South Lake wooden directional post.

Giant redwood Wellingtonia trees,
azaleas, berberis, rowans, North American
conifers and a host of alpine and
moorland shrubs all feature in Cragside's
thousand acres.

Go on past the caves and rocky outcrops
and turn right at the top of the hill, again
following the South Lake sign. Continue
past the small Slipper Lake (Tarn) and
turn left to follow the South Lake sign on

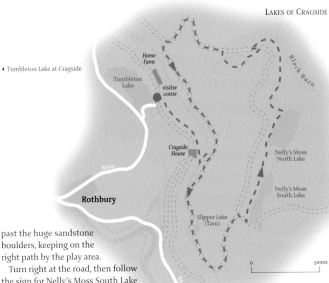

◄ Tumbleton Lake at Cragside

past the huge sandstone boulders, keeping on the right path by the play area.

Turn right at the road, then follow the sign for Nelly's Moss South Lake by the stone steps to the left. Carry on along the waterside by the natural rock path up to the North Lake and on to the wooden bridge over the burn.

Turn left immediately, following the path signed for the flume. Follow the wooden flume as it winds its way around above the pretty gorge of the Black Burn.

At the end of the flume follow the path for the Canada Car Park to the left, then follow the wooden signpost for Canada Drive. At the telephone mast turn right, following the sign for Moorside car park through the dense woodland, keeping on the right-hand path down to the picnic tables. Follow the level tarmac one-way road to the left and on until you reach the signpost for Middle Drive and turn left back onto the woodland trail.

Stay on the high path at the sign for Basin Tank Tarn and carry on to the deep, black pool. Approximately 100 yards past the tarn, turn right down the stone steps leading back down to Crozier Drive above the house.

There is plenty left to explore before returning to the car park; don't miss the rock garden below the house, the largest in Europe, or the spectacular view from the iron bridge. The house itself is a fascinating place to tour and there is a busy programme of exhibitions and seasonal events. Over the iron bridge, the Victorian formal gardens, with great views of the Simonside Hills and Coquetdale, are a short walk away.

Selby's Cove and Simonside

Distance 6.5km **Time** 2 hours 30
Terrain stone and rough tracks with
bogland, heather and a steep ascent
Map OS Explorer OL42 **Access**
summertime bus service (508) between
Rothbury and Morpeth. Car park at
Lordenshaws, 1.6km off the B6342, 3km
south of Rothbury

Take a more demanding detour off the
popular route up Simonside to explore the
remote sandstone outcrop of Selby's Cove.
The Selbys were a notorious Reiver family
and this sheltered spot is said to have been
their favoured hideout.

The walk begins at the Lordenshaws car
park in the shadow of the Simonside Hills.
Before crossing the road and setting off up
the hill it is worth exploring the

mysterious cup and ring marked rocks and
Iron Age hillfort of Lordenshaws which is a
short walk across the exposed moorland.
There's a small stone burial cist on the
lower left bank of the fort which is difficult
to find but worth exploring; swords, flint
tools and pottery have all been unearthed
at the site.

After returning to the car park, take
the signposted and paved path up
Simonside's heather-clad slopes. It's a
steady climb up to a split where most
walkers will follow the path up to the top
of the Simonside ridge. However, this
route follows the St Oswald's Way trail in
reverse down to the left past the former
shepherd's cottage at Spylaw. Following
this line takes you over some boggy
marshland near the Forest Burn to reach

the Coquet Cairn, the highest point on the 156km-long St Oswald's Way.

After following the treeline for a short distance, turn north past the ruins of an old farmstead to reach the rocky outcrops at Selby's Cove. This secluded spot is popular with rock climbers but its sheltered grey stone faces and scree slopes are nonetheless always spookily silent and calm whatever winds are howling over the peaks of Simonside.

From here, it's a boot-straining yomp over the heather and rough grasses as you follow the treeline to eventually reach a steep worn soil and rock track which takes you up to the summit of Simonside.

If the weather is with you then your efforts will be well-rewarded with breathtaking views of the Cheviots and into Scotland, up the Coquet Valley and out to the coast at Blyth. You can even see the cranes on the River Tyne at Wallsend from Simonside on a clear day. As the hills are visible from out at sea, 'seaman's sight' is one suggestion for the origins of the hill's name.

This is also deepest 'duergar' country. In Northumberland folklore these malevolent dwarfs – also known as 'brownmen' or 'bogles' – enjoy leading unwary walkers over the edge of the Simonside cliffs. In truth, you're more likely to come across one of the wild mountain goats that live here.

You may also spot birds of prey such as buzzards or kestrels, and deer and red squirrels inhabit the surrounding forests on the slopes of the sandstone ridge.

From the cairn at the summit head east back down the path to Dove Crag and rejoin the trail where you initially split off back down to Lordenshaws.

◀ The path from Lordenshaws

Otterburn

Kielder Water

④
②
③

Cambo

① Bellingham

⑤ ⑥
⑦ ⑧
Haltwhistle

Hayden
Bridge

⑨ Hexham
⑩

Hadrian's Wall is the most popular tourist attraction in the north of England and the historic town of Hexham in the heart of Tynedale is an excellent base for exploring the area around the World Heritage Site. With the huge forest park at Kielder Water not far away to the northwest it's not surprising this area attracts scores of walkers.

This section begins with a classic out-and-back from the town of Bellingham up a tree-lined gorge to a beautiful waterfall. More remote is a circular tour of fortified houses built in the days when no-one was safe from the lawless Border Reivers.

At Kielder Water the next pair of walks show two different sides of the landscape. The first follows the southern shore on an easy path between visitor centres with a return by ferry. The second heads up the hillside to a recent addition to the park which draws stargazers from far and wide.

Stretching 120km from Wallsend in the east to Bowness-on-Solway in the west with milecastles, turrets and garrisons along the way, the next three walks take in the most interesting parts of Hadrian's great wall. The first visits a reclaimed quarry and an excellent section of the wall as it follows the undulating landscape. The next takes you to two of the most important garrison sites and the third follows the burn up from Haltwhistle for a different approach.

Towards Hexham, the next walk is a lovely stroll in a landscaped gorge not far from the busy A69. In Hexham itself you can take a leisurely tour to the spot where the rivers of the North and South Tyne meet up before heading off to Newcastle and the sea at Tynemouth. Finally, you can enjoy a local beauty spot – and scene of a terrible military disaster in the Wars of the Roses – just south of the town.

Kielder, Hadrian's Wall and Hexham

Hareshaw Linn

Distance 5km Time 2 hours
Terrain compact gravel tracks, stone
steps with some steep steps
Map OS Explorer OL42 Access car park
(free) in Bellingham. Regular bus (880)
from Hexham

This popular out and back walk from
Bellingham takes you alongside the
Hareshaw Burn through an ancient
woodland to a beautiful waterfall which
enchanted Victorian tourists.

Bellingham is 15km from Kielder
Water Forest Park. The car park for this
walk is opposite the local garage, just
over the bridge in the centre of the village
(the bridge is across the road from the
police station).

Turn right by the information board
and follow the wooden fingerpost signed

for Hareshaw Linn up the path by the
burn, going through the wooden kissing
gate by the farm outbuildings.

Pass the caravan park on your right
and head uphill on the waymarked path
to the first waterfall at the site of the
19th-century Hareshaw Ironworks.

At its peak there were two blast
furnaces in operation here, as well as 70
coke ovens, 24 roasting kilns and various
store buildings, stables and sheds. The
works closed down in 1848 and nature
quickly reclaimed the valley. Today
Hareshaw is a Site of Special Scientific
Interest(SSSI) and more than 300 different
types of lichen, mosses and liverworts can
be found in the area.

Continue on the path uphill to a picnic
area, then follow the steps up by the
wooden waymarker signed for the

◀ Bridge over the Hareshaw Burn

waterfall. Go through the next wooden gate and onto the stone trail into the woodland high above the burn. Keep following the path as it carries on along the right bank through the ash, elm and oak trees of Blakelaw Plantation.

The path goes uphill at some steps by a curved stone seat, then down to where you cross the burn over a wooden bridge. Continue to your right on the path up the left bank and past the curved wooden seat, known as 'Cupid's Bower' with a small waterfall running down to your left.

The stone steps take you down past a wooden handrail and on alongside the fast-flowing water. Cross a second wooden bridge back over to the right bank and continue north to a third wooden bridge back over to the left bank. The path goes on through the picturesque woodland in a high-sided gorge and over a fourth wooden bridge into more open trees, including huge Douglas firs.

Carry on through the bracken, over a fifth bridge, and up the stone steps and wooden walkway to a crossed timber bridge above a pretty waterfall. On summer evenings, picnics, music recitals and other entertainments were enjoyed here by Victorian visitors.

Cross the bridge and continue up the path on the left to the high ivy-

covered outcrops and the Hareshaw Linn waterfall itself. After enjoying the racing water, turn around and retrace your steps down to Bellingham.

Black Middens and the Reivers Trail

Distance **5km** Time **2 hours**
Terrain **waymarked grass and forest
paths** Map **OS Explorer OL42** Access **car
park (free) at Black Middens. No public
transport**

**Explore North Tynedale's troubled
past on this atmospheric walk through
Reiver history.**

Park in the Black Middens Bastle car
park just beyond Greenhaugh and
Gatehouse, 4km northwest of
Bellingham (follow the brown roadsigns).

Before setting off on the walk, go
through the wooden gate by the Reivers
Trail information point and head up the
field to the roofless Black Middens, the
best preserved bastle in Tarset Burn.

The bastle is a 16th-century defensive
farmhouse for the clan and their livestock
with thick impenetrable walls and a

removable staircase to the upstairs
living quarters. This area was frequently
troubled by raiders from over the border
but the men of Tarset also gained a
formidable reputation of their own and
their cry of 'Tarset and Tarret Burn, hard
and heather bred, yet-yet-yet' was often
heard on moonlit nights in the glens of
lowland Scotland.

Return to the car park and follow the
road to the right and on up to the
concrete bridge at Waterhead Cottage.
Turn left and cross the bridge, then bear
right and follow the red waymarker up
the forestry road and into the trees.

Stick to the red waymarkers that lead

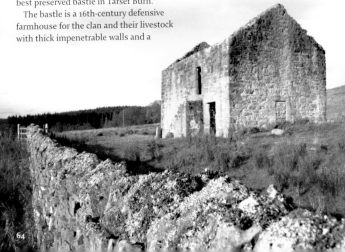

Bastle (ruins)

Bastle (ruins)

Comb

Blacklinn Burn

Waterhead

Black Middens

Shipley Shiels

0   500m

Gleedlee

To Greenhaugh & Bellingham

Tarset Burn

Sidwood

you off the road and onto a grass track to your right. Carry on up to Starr Head Bastle at Shilla Hill, once the home of Hodge Corbett, nicknamed Corbett Jack.

Explore the remains, then head to the right by the information point on the track that descends into the tree cover to the next red trail marker.

The path goes on through the trees and crosses a burn. Stay with the red arrow markers as the path runs between the woods and the sparkling Tarset Burn before going left up the shingle steps into the conifers. Carry on following the burn until you reach Corbie Castle at Bog Head. This was the home of Barty Milburn, a notorious local hard man who is said to have killed two Scots after taking back some stolen sheep from a raiding gang. In the skirmish, Barty was wounded, his sidekick Corbett Jack killed and, in Barty's own words, the head of one of the unfortunate Reivers 'sprang alang the heather like an onion'.

Head into the woods by the waymarker, before turning left out onto the forestry road. Follow the waymarked road over the moorland before taking the fork to the left to return to Waterhead Cottage.

Turn right over the wooden bridge and follow the red waymarker past the cottage. Follow the path running to the left down by the burn to the grassed-over ruin of Wood House Bastle.

Keep on the path and go over the footbridge down on your left before crossing the field to reach a bend in the road. Turn left on the road to return to the Black Middens car park.

◀ Black Middens bastle house

Kielder Water and Bull Crag

**Distance 11km Time 3 hours (one way)
Terrain good paths, forest tracks
Map OS Explorer OL42 Access car park
(pay and display) at Tower Knowe
Visitor Centre. Return by ferry**

With almost 45km of shoreline and 600
square kilometres of forest, Kielder Water
and its Forest Park is one vast adventure
playground. This walk between visitor
centres on the southern shore is a good
introduction to its charms. This is a linear
route so it's advisable to book the return
ferry before you set off.

This walk starts off from Tower
Knowe Visitor Centre, one of three on the
lakeside and the first one you come to by
the C200 road from Bellingham. Head
west along the Lakeside Way signposted
for Leaplish Waterside. The trail is
designed to be used by cyclists, horse
riders, mobility scooters and wheelchair
users as well as walkers. The north shore
has no visitor centres so is a lot less busy
than the south shore.

After 1km there is a sign for the Elf Kirk
viewpoint. This short detour across the
road and up a little hill gives you a good
view of the lake, as well as an opportunity
to see the peninsula of Bull Crag ahead.

Back on the trail, pass the moored boats
at the Little Whickhope inlet and carry on
the winding path towards Bull Crag,
passing over Cranecleugh Burn as it runs
into the lake. There is an option to turn
left here to shorten the walk and bypass
the peninsula, but you would miss much
of the Kielder Keepsake Trail if you did.
This is a series of bronze rubbing plaques
created by artist Nicola Moss; you can buy
a pack with the equipment to make the
rubbings from the visitor centre. These
artworks are just one part of the biggest
outdoor art project in the country; an

◄ Kielder Water

initiative which has been running at Kielder since 1995.

Carry on right past the car park to enjoy the views back to Tower Knowe and the massive dam as you walk around the headland. The enigmatic concrete structure in the lake in front of the dam is the Valve Tower which controls the flow of water back to the North Tyne River. Kielder Water is the biggest artificial lake in the UK and was created in the 1980s to support the needs of industry on the Tyne. It was criticised by many as a white elephant after construction as the traditional industries which would have used the water went into decline soon after the valley floor was flooded.

Turning back inland you soon come to a leftover section of the old valley road, the rest of it now under the water. Carry on along the shoreline path to the Otterstone Viewpoint and back inland, looking out for Freya's Cabin, a shelter made from layers of shaped wooden profiles. Part of the artworks programe, it was made to tell the imagined story of Freya and Robin, two lovers separated by the lake. Robin's Hut is directly opposite on the north shore.

Bear right shortly after the cabin to follow the path to Leaplish Waterside Park where you can also visit the excellent Bird of Prey Centre before catching the ferry back to the start.

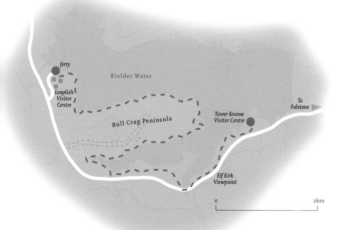

Kielder Observatory

Distance 3.5km **Time** 1 hour 30 (one way)
Terrain steadily climbing ascent on
compact surface through forestry land
Map OS Explorer OL42 **Access** car park at
Kielder Castle Visitor Centre

Kielder is such a remote spot on the
western frontier of Northumberland that
it enjoys the lowest light pollution in
England, making it the perfect place to
watch the stars. This walk from Kielder
Village takes you up forested hillside to
the Kielder Observatory, a very modern
structure which sits perfectly in this
'dark sky' landscape.

Kielder Village was originally created by
the Forestry Commission to house
workers employed to plant trees in the
1940s and '50s. The village was connected
to Hexham by rail but the line was closed
and the last passenger train left Forest
Station in 1956; the old station, next to
the community-owned garage, is now a
private house.

From the car park at Kielder Castle
Visitor Centre follow the road around
and back out onto the C200. Cross the
road at the garage and bike-hire shop and
turn left to pick up the waymarked trail
heading up into the forest.

Continue up the path through the trees
to reach a more open forest road and
eventually the rocky outcrop of Cat Cairn,
said to be the home of the last, now
extinct, wildcats in Northumberland.
Looking back down you can see the huge
Kielder Water reservoir, formed by
damming and flooding the valley,
surrounded by the largest man-made
woodland in Europe – there are thought
to be some 155 million trees planted here.
More than half the red squirrel population
of England can be found in this forest.

The circular stone 'Skyspace' building
with a large concrete tunnel entrance was
designed by American artist James Turrell
and is one of 40 similarly-themed
temporary and permanent installations

made by him around the world since 1974. Inside, your focus is on the sky seen through a circular opening in the roof of the dome; at dawn and dusk a solar lighting system illuminates the inside of the chamber. It is very easy to spend longer than intended here, contemplating the sky and the universe above you.

Carry on up the hillside, past the mountain bike trail and up the last stiff incline to reach an open area of felled woodland and the observatory.

Set on concrete stilts and powered by wind and the sun, the observatory was designed by London-based architect Charles Barclay and is managed by the Kielder Observatory Astronomical Society. These volunteers also organise the many public talks

and demonstrations held here throughout the year, as well as the Kielder Forest Star Camp every autumn. (The observatory is not manned full-time, so you need to check with the Society for upcoming events if you would like to see the telescopes housed in the two hand-cranked turrets in operation.)

Without going inside, however, you can enjoy this wonderful location and take a stroll on the timber terrace of the observatory, enjoying the view as the steady whip of the wind turbine punctuates the air. Return to Kielder Village the way you came.

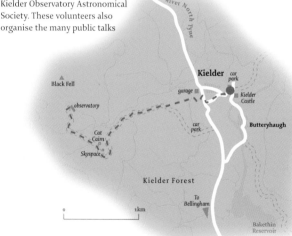

Walltown Quarry and the Nine Nicks

Distance 3km **Time** 1 hour 30
Terrain roadside, compact chippings
paths, grass tracks **Map** OS Explorer OL43
Access car park at the Roman Army
Museum just off the B6318 near
Greenhead. Bus (AD122) from Carlisle and
Newcastle. The trails around Walltown
quarry are wheelchair/buggy accessible,
but the section of the wall is not

**Learn what life was like for Legionnaires
serving Rome on the wildest frontier of
the empire with a visit to the Roman
Army Museum, then explore one of the
best-preserved sections of Hadrian's Wall.**

Set off from the Roman Army Museum
on the path past the car park and turn left
down the roadside to reach Walltown
Quarry on your right. (There are toilets
and a coffee shop here.) Before being

reclaimed by the National Parks
Authority, whinstone was quarried here
and used as chippings in the tarmac
which covers many of Britain's roads.

Follow the yellow waymarked trail past
the stacks of igneous rock at Rabbit
Heugh on your left and Quarry Lake down
to your right. The trail rises gently to the
right as you head towards the crags. Turn
left through the kissing gate and head up
the grassy hillside, following the drystone
wall. It's a short, steep rise up to the top,
but well worth it for the fantastic views
back down over the old quarry and the
surrounding countryside. Keep on past
the craggy outcrops to reach Hadrian's
Wall straight ahead.

The wall was begun in AD122 during the
reign of Emperor Hadrian and was the
first of two great defensive walls built

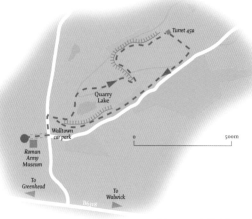

across Britain (the other being the less well-preserved Antonine Wall across central Scotland). Although heavily fortified, the wall is thought by historians to have been of most importance as a symbol of Roman power; the completed walls would have been plastered and whitewashed to reflect the sun, making it visible from many miles away.

Built with great skill, this section of the wall goes over a series of hills known as the Nine Nicks of Thirlwall, although thanks to the quarry, there are now only seven.

Continue east with the wall over a few tricky dolerite boulders as the path rises and falls, soon coming to an excellent vantage point at Turret 45a. These look-out posts were spaced out between the larger milecastles, usually three of them to every mile, and were manned by small detachments of soldiers. Turret 45a is

unusual, however, in that it was built as a watchtower before the wall.

Beyond the turret the fabric of the wall starts to deteriorate, so after admiring the views across the 'barbarian' land to the north and across to Steel Rigg in the east, bear south away from the turret down the hill on the worn grass path to the car park beside the woods.

Turn right at the bottom of the hill just before the car park and head along the grass trail in the field, which is part of the Pennine Way National Trail. Cross the cattle grid at the road and turn right through the wooden gate into woodland. Take the low path running along the roadside through the bracken and trees to a second wooden gate at a small stone bridge. Go through the gate and up the steep stone steps by the public footpath fingerpost. The path bears right past a wooden seat and comes out at the quarry car park.

◀ Hadrian's Wall east of Walltown Quarry

71

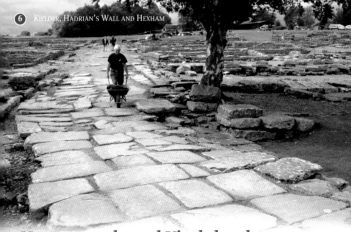

Housesteads and Vindolanda

Distance 12km Time 4 hours
Terrain tarmac roads, grass tracks, worn
pathways, stone steps and steep ascents
and descents unsuitable for buggies
Map OS Explorer OL43 Access trains to
Carlisle and Hexham with connecting
bus service (AD122) to Once Brewed,
Housesteads and Vindolanda

This half-day circular hike takes in one of
the most scenic parts of Hadrian's Wall
and visits the most complete Roman
forts in the country.

From the National Park Visitor Centre at
Once Brewed follow the B6318 Military
Road north towards Steel Rigg. Once
Brewed got its name because the workers
who built the military road reckoned the
beer served in the local hostelry was so
weak that it needed to be brewed twice.
When the hostel opened nearby the
teetotal owner only served tea, just

brewed once, and the name stuck.

Follow the road steadily uphill, then
turn right through the kissing gate just
past Peel Bothy cottage onto the
signposted public footpath that leads you
to Hadrian's Wall at Peel Crags. Cross the
field, then climb the wooden fence to
reach the remains of a turret. Head right
up the stone steps and on to the ridge,
following the line of the wall.

Cross the stile and continue to follow
the wall as you come down off Peel Crags,
then carry on up the grass slope with
views down to Crag Lough. Go down
again to reach Milecastle 39 – 'Castle Nick'
– a barracks for around 20 soldiers.

Keep following the wall to the next
sharp descent at Sycamore Gap, a spot
made famous in the movie *Robin Hood,
Prince of Thieves*. Cross the wall here and
continue to climb east, following the laid
stone trail, looking back to see the natural

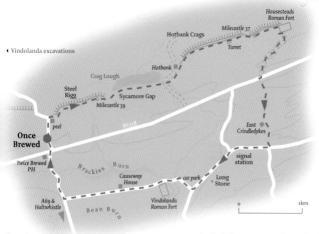

◄ Vindolanda excavations

frontier created by the **Whin Sill**.

Go over the wooden stile and keep on with Crag Lough below you (be careful to keep away from the edge). Pass through the pleasant wooded area and follow the track until you reach a wooden signpost for Housesteads. Go through the gate and follow the track up past Hotbank Farm to Hotbank Crags. There is another dip down tricky stone steps onto Housesteads Crags before you reach Milecastle 37 with the remains of an arched doorway. Carry on through the wooden gate and cross the field to come out at the entrance of Housesteads.

Detour to explore the fort and museum (entry fee) or carry on the walk by heading downhill and following the track to the right past the farmhouse. Keep on the track until you reach the Military Road.

Cross the road to follow the waymarked public bridleway south over the fields to East Crindledykes Farm. Go through the gates left of the farm and continue south on the tarmac road. Turn right at the top of the hill and head west along the road passing the Long Stone signalling station on the hilltop to your left. Carry on along the road until you come to the signpost for Vindolanda.

Built to guard the Stanegate, the Roman road from the Tyne to the Solway, the fort of Vindolanda is best known for the tablet letters uncovered here which provide a fascinating insight into ordinary domestic life on the frontier of the Roman Empire.

From Vindolanda follow the road on past the main entrance and the heather-thatched Causeway Cottage. The remains of a Roman milestone can be seen off to the left as you come to the end of the road. Turn right at the junction to return to Once Brewed.

Haltwhistle Burn to Cawfields

Distance 10km **Time** 3 hours 30
Terrain rough tracks, tarmac paths and
pavements, grass tracks with steep
ascents at Hadrian's Wall **Map** OS
Explorer OL43 **Access** good road and rail
transport links to Haltwhistle. Hadrian's
Wall Country bus service (AD122) runs
from Newcastle to Carlisle (April to
October)

**Follow the peaty waters of the
Haltwhistle Burn through woodland and
exposed rockfaces up to Hadrian's Wall
and back on this hike.**

Haltwhistle is a quiet town today, but in
1598 a band of notorious Liddesdale
Armstrongs swept into the marketplace
and fired houses, murdered and captured
residents and drove off cattle in broad
daylight. When the flames had burned
out, the English March Warden led a
retaliatory raid and Sim Armstrong of the
Cathill was killed by one of the local
Ridleys. The Armstrongs hit back and

when clan leader Wat Armstrong was
shot through the eye by a longbow arrow
fired by Alec Ridley, it led to a long-
running feud between the two families.
There are a couple of old bastle houses
from that time still standing near the
Centre of Britain Hotel (the town being
the midway point between Land's End
and John O'Groats).

Set out from the railway station,
crossing the bridge and turning left past
the smart old signal box down the ramp.
Continue through the trees and along the
path by the banks of the South Tyne, past
the Kilfrost factory and on to Alston
Arches Viaduct.

Follow the wooden signpost for
Townfoot through the metal stile and
continue along the beautiful banks of the
river under the roadbridge. Go through
the kissing gate and follow the narrow
track over the grass.

Near where the Haltwhistle Burn runs
into the river, turn left and follow it

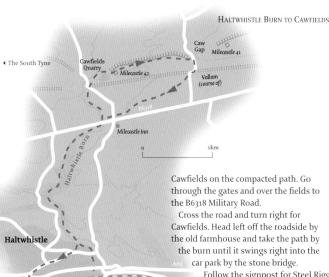

The South Tyne ◄

Caw Gap

Milecastle 41

Cawfields Quarry

Milecastle 42

Vallum (course of)

B6318

Milecastle Inn

0 1km

Haltwhistle

viaduct

River South Tyne

A69

Cawfields on the compacted path. Go through the gates and over the fields to the B6318 Military Road.

Cross the road and turn right for Cawfields. Head left off the roadside by the old farmhouse and take the path by the burn until it swings right into the car park by the stone bridge.

Follow the signpost for Steel Rigg out of the car park, past the small tarn at the old quarry and up onto the ridge and Hadrian's Wall. Head east along the Roman fortifications past Milecastle 42 and on for 1.6km to Caw Gap. At the roadside turn right, then right again at the signpost for Milecastle Inn. Head diagonally across the field up onto the brow towards the Military Road.

Cross the stile and turn right past the Inn, then retrace your footsteps back down Haltwhistle Burn. At the houses turn right up Mill Lane onto High Row and go up the steep hill past Castle Hill Terrace. Follow the signs back down into the town centre past the Grey Bull pub. When you come to the War Memorial Hospital on your right, bear left down Westgate and the train station is directly in front of you.

upstream. Go under the roadbridge, then through the metal gate and under Lady's Lonnen Bridge. Take care while crossing the busy road, then follow the track signed for Townfoot to the right of the industrial estate. Accompany the burn past the old brewery and mill and up the cobbled street to the bottom of Castle Hill.

Cross the road and continue on the path by the burn until you reach a white-railed footbridge by a row of old miners' cottages. Don't cross the bridge, but continue along the burn, past a cottage and on through the trees to a second white bridge. Cross and carry on following the waterside and the footpath signs for

Bardon Mill and Allen Banks

**Distance 10km Time 3 hours
Terrain roadside, grass tracks,
waymarked woodland and riverside
tracks with high gorge sides
Map OS Explorer OL43 Access good train
links to Bardon Mill from Carlisle and
Newcastle. Arriva bus (685) to and from
Carlisle and Newcastle**

**Take a half-day hike from the village of
Bardon Mill to a popular National Trust
beauty spot alongside the River Allen.**

Start out from the Bowes Hotel in
Bardon Mill, heading right through the
village past the pottery, the last in Britain
licensed to produce salt glaze pottery.

Cross the narrow stone bridge and turn
right past the war memorial by Ashcroft
Farm and down to the railway crossing
gates, signed for Allen Banks.

Continue on the path heading
southeast. Go over the metal footbridge
crossing the deep South Tyne and turn
left onto the quiet country road.

This leads you to the church and small
green in the centre of the tiny village of
Beltingham where you head right, then
immediately left, down the gravel track
signed for Ridley Bridge and Allen Bank.
Take the footpath into the woods,
following the yellow waymarker, to the
kissing gate at the end of a metal fence.

Continue on up the field, with the fence
on your right, to the kissing gate at the
road. Turn right uphill and go past Ridley
Bastle House, dating back to the early
1600s, then after a double bend in the
road, drop downhill past the farm silo and
turn left onto a path signed for Allen
Banks Estate.

Follow the yellow waymarkers to reach
the metal National Trust sign at Allen
Banks. Go over the stile here and turn
right up the yellow waymarked track,

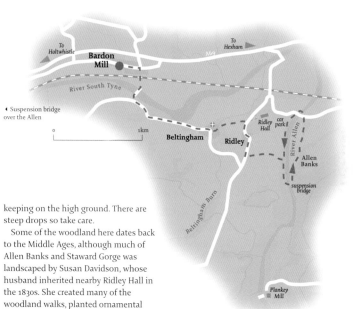

◀ Suspension bridge over the Allen

keeping on the high ground. There are steep drops so take care.

Some of the woodland here dates back to the Middle Ages, although much of Allen Banks and Staward Gorge was landscaped by Susan Davidson, whose husband inherited nearby Ridley Hall in the 1830s. She created many of the woodland walks, planted ornamental as well as conifer trees and built summerhouses and a wigwam.

Follow the trail steeply uphill to the wooden summer house (a reconstruction of the Victorian original) and bear right to continue on the orange waymarked track. At the next orange waymarker, head left steeply down the footpath, then left again following the river trail into the gorge. (For a longer walk, turn right here instead and head up to the bridge at Plankey Mill, following the black waymarkers.)

Continue left to the next yellow waymarker, taking the right track by the river to a suspension footbridge. Cross the river and turn left, going through two stiles along the edge of the fields, with the river on your left.

Go under the roadbridge and turn right to cross over the metal bridge. Take care of traffic as you follow the road back to Allen Banks car park.

Head through the car park and take the track bearing right uphill just past the wooden waymarker. Go up the wooden steps and continue along the gorge back to the stile and metal sign where you entered the woods. Retrace your steps to Bardon Mill.

The Meeting of the Waters

Distance 7.2km Time 2 hours
Terrain flat woodland tracks, tarmac
paths and pavements. All-terrain buggy
friendly Map OS Explorer OL43
Access good road and rail transport links
to Hexham. Regular trains and buses
from Carlisle and Newcastle

This looping tour of the historic market
town of Hexham takes in Tyne Green
Country Park and visits the meeting
point of the South and North Tyne Rivers.

Hexham's Old Gaol is the first recorded
purpose-built prison in England and was
constructed in 1333 by order of the
Archbishop of York. His bailiff and
officials controlled Hexhamshire from
the nearby Moot Hall. Today, the Old Gaol
is a visitor attraction, complete with
stocks at the door, which tells the story
of the Border Reivers often imprisoned
there in vivid colour.

Set out on your walk from the Old Gaol
and head left, following the sign for
Wentworth car park down the lane
signposted for the railway station.

Cross the road and continue on the
path past the running track, keeping
on the left side of the road as it goes on
past the leisure centre. Cross at the
roundabout and turn right to go over
the bridge.

At the next roundabout turn left,
following the signpost for Tyne Green
Country Park and pick up the waterside
path to your left by the slow-running
River Tyne, dark as brown ale. Walk on
through the avenue of trees past the
children's playpark and beside the golf
course. The track joins a tarmac footpath
running next to the railway line; continue
to head west along it.

As the river bends, turn right at the
wooden public footpath sign and take the

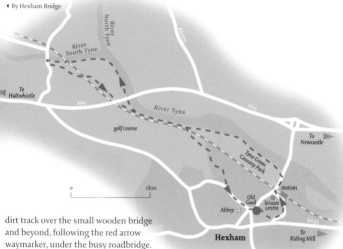

◄ By Hexham Bridge

dirt track over the small wooden bridge and beyond, following the red arrow waymarker, under the busy roadbridge.

Accompany the Tyne to the point where the South and North Tyne Rivers meet. The South Tyne flows from Alston Moor in Cumbria and the North from Kielder Water close to the Scottish Border.

Stay on the track as it swings up onto the road at West Boat and go past Yew Tree Cottage, following the road back towards Hexham. Turn left under the railway bridge and follow the blue cycleway sign east under the road flyover again. Rejoin the tarmac track heading back to Tyne Green.

At the railway crossing point, just before you re-enter the park by the golf course, go through the metal gate and cross the wooden sleepers, following the sign for Chareway Lane.

The path leads you alongside the sandstone wall and past the caravans to come out onto the road at the bus depot. Turn right onto Chareway and you'll see the clockfaces of the abbey up to your right.

Carry on up Gilesgate to Market Place and the abbey, which dominates the town. Although founded by St Wilfred in the 7th century, most of the building you see today dates from the 12th century. The original Benedictine crypt of St Wilfred remains, however, and can be reached through the current nave. The park behind the abbey, with its charming bandstand, is also worth visiting before you return to the start.

Swallowship Pool

Distance 3.5km **Time** 1 hour 30
Terrain roadside, compacted woodland
roads and dirt tracks **Map OS Explorer
OL43 Access** limited parking in lay-by on
B6306 beside Kingswood Education &
Outdoor centre. Good regular rail and bus
links to Hexham from Carlisle and
Newcastle

**This woodland walk takes you to a deep
fishing pool and beauty spot on the
evocatively-named Devil's Water just to
the south of Hexham.**

Start from the small lay-by beside the
Kingswood Education and Outdoor
Centre north of Linnels Bridge on the
B6306. When locals pass over the humped
bridge it is customary for them to lift
both feet off the floor; the river crossed is
the Devil's Water after all.

Head north up the roadside a short
distance to North Lodge House and take
the path into the woods, following the
public footpath signpost. Continue east
along the compacted gravel surface.

Look out for an old walnut tree on the
left just before Garden Cottage. It is said
to mark the site where Henry Beaufort,
3rd Duke of Somerset, was captured
following his defeat at the Battle of
Hexham in 1464. Surprisingly little is
recorded about the battle, but it is
thought that the Lancastrian camp near
Linnels Bridge was taken by surprise as
the Yorkists quickly crossed the Tyne to
advance on Hexham. In a chaotic retreat
many men drowned in the Devil's Water
or were crushed as they tried to scramble
up the steep riverbank.

The Duke was quickly executed on the
evening of the battle, along with 30 other
leading Lancastrians, in the town's

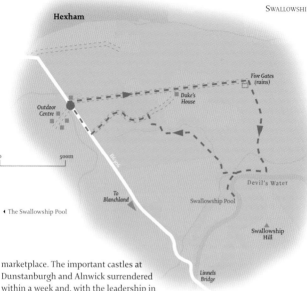

Hexham

Outdoor
Centre

Duke's
House

Five Gates
(ruins)

500m

To
Blanchland

Swallowship Pool

Devil's Water

Swallowship
Hill

Linnels
Bridge

◂ The Swallowship Pool

marketplace. The important castles at
Dunstanburgh and Alnwick surrendered
within a week and, with the leadership in
the north shattered, the Wars of the Roses
came to an end – for a few years at least.

Continue past the Duke's House, an
impressive neo-gothic mansion with lots
of chimney pots, until you reach a fork in
the path near the hidden ruins of Five
Gates House. Go right and watch out for
the huge wood ant nests made from pine
needles alongside the rooty trail. The ants
shoot formic acid from their rear end if
disturbed – best to leave well alone.
Roe deer are also seen in the woods,
though not as often now as in the past.

The trail curves through Scots pines as
it makes its way south. Go right when the
path ends at a junction and follow the
path high above the Devil's Water until
you see a well-worn track dropping down

by the side of a burn. It can be a bit tricky
here – it is steep and there are slippery
exposed tree roots – but it is worth it for
the view that awaits; the Swallowship
Pool with the sandstone walls of the
gorge reflecting in its still waters.

Explore around the pool, then retrace
your steps back up the side of the burn.
At the main path bear north to pick up the
yellow waymarked trail through the
woods. Turn left at the signpost for
Hexham Road, going past the huge
red-barked Wellingtonia trees and
rhododendron bushes on the way. Follow
the path out onto the road at the
Kingdom Hall and turn right to return
to the start point.

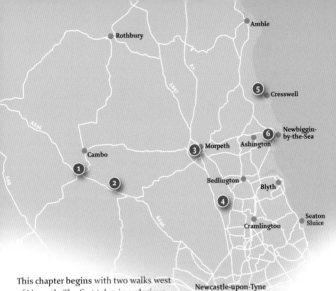

This chapter begins with two walks west of Morpeth. The first takes in a glorious country house and its landscaped gardens on an easy-going stroll. The second leaves from a clay-lined lake to follow farm tracks and field paths up to some interesting geology and fine views.

Morpeth has suffered less from historical border conflict than other Northumbrian towns further north, but has a castle that was built in the 13th century on the site of earlier fortifications. A circular walk visits the castle as well as passing the town's abbey, which wasn't so fortunate and now lies in ruins.

The area east of Morpeth formed the bulk of the former Northumberland coalfield which at its peak employed 227,000 miners in 70 working collieries and shaped a great deal of the political and social attitudes of the region. Now

there are none, but land reclaimed provides new opportunities for walkers.

The fourth walk is a quick getaway in a lovely woodland park; an oasis in a busy part of the county. Further north and heading up the coast, the sands of Druridge Bay stretch on for miles. The walk here visits the dunes and beach as well as nature reserves popular with birdwatchers. Down from these quiet havens, the final walk sets off from the town once called 'the biggest mining village in the world' and goes through new parkland to an excellent mining museum before delivering you at the sea, where an enigmatic piece of sculpture stops you in your tracks.

Morpeth and the southeast

Wallington Hall

Distance 4.5km **Time** 2 hours
Terrain compacted woodland and
riverside trails, muddy tracks and a set of
stepping stones **Map** OS Explorer OL29
Access limited Arriva bus service (419)
from Morpeth. Car Park (free) at
Wallington Hall, B6342 1.6km south of
Cambo. Entry fee for house and grounds
except for National Trust members

Wallington Hall is a 17th-century house,
surrounded by beautiful gardens and
parkland, given to the National Trust by
Sir Charles Philipps Trevelyan in 1942.
This short walk is a treat for wildlife
lovers: look out for otters, red squirrels
and woodpeckers.

Walk through the entrance at the
clocktower and turn right at the Hall,
following the path by the broad lawns
with views over the Wansbeck Valley.

At the ornate urn at the end of the path
follow the sign to the right, taking the
path into the West Wood. Go past the old
icehouse on your left then bear right at
the fork leading up to the wildlife hide.

Follow the path to the left at the sign
for the hide and cross the small wooden
bridge, continuing on the path to the
right. At the hide you can watch out for
red squirrels at the feeders and other
elusive Northumberland wildlife.

Head back down the path, turning onto
the trail that you came up, until you reach
the sign for the River Walk; turn right over
the small wooden walkway into the trees.

Continue on the tranquil path to the
edge of the West Wood and go on down as
it swings to the left through the bracken.
Turn right at the stone wall and five-bar
gate, following the path down to the
River Wansbeck.

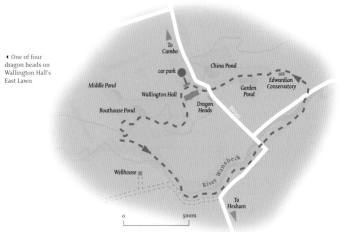

◄ One of four dragon heads on Wallington Hall's East Lawn

Keep to the path alongside the water to the green wooden bridge. Cross over and turn left to continue on the path through the woods to the humped roadbridge. Pass under the first stone arch and cross the wooden stile, heading straight on by the permissive footpath at the water's edge.

Follow the path through the fields, then take care to cross the river at the stepping stones. Pass through the first kissing gate and head straight up to the second.

Cross the road and follow the sign for the walled garden, bearing right through the metal gate. The track leads you alongside a field, under a tangle of small trees, to a wall with a wooden gate. Skirt to the right on the path and go over the stone steps in the wall.

Go straight on past the back of the Edwardian conservatory and take the path to the right at the Garden Pond, then follow the fork to the left as you re-enter the woods.

This path leads to a metal gate at the main road. Take care of the traffic and cross back into the Hall grounds at the set of metal gates on the other side. Follow the path back round to the start.

It's well worth taking the time to explore more of Wallington Hall and its grounds before making your way back to the car park. As well as the walled garden, café and adventure playground with a 12m-long play train, which children will love, there are great collections of furniture, books, family portraits, pre-Raphaelite paintings (including eight large wall paintings by William Bell Scott which capture 2000 years of local history), toy soldiers, doll's houses and an extraordinary Cabinet of Curiosities.

Bolam Lake and Shaftoe Crags

Distance 12km **Time** 3 hours 30
Terrain compacted woodland trails,
wooden walkways, field paths, farm
tracks and country roads
Map OS Explorer 325 **Access** no public
transport to Bolam. Car park (pay and
display) with facilities at the Boat House

**Bolam Lake Country Park is the starting
point for this signposted circular route
through fine Northumberland
countryside which takes in some weird
and wonderful rock formations and
great views.**

From the Bolam Low House car park
(pay and display) go out onto the road
and head right towards the junction.
Carry on along the road for a short
distance before entering the field on
your right by Bolam Low House.

Cross the field to reach a wooden
bridge, then follow the field edge to the
ladder stile at Curlybog Plantation. Go
through the trees to another stile and

bear right after joining the track. Go
through the gates and over the
footbridge, then cross the field towards
Sandyford Farm. Bear left when you reach
the road and carry on past the house at
West Tofthill.

Before you reach the A696, turn right at
the sign for the peel tower of East Shaftoe
Hall. Follow the path along the field
divide and turn left before the hall onto
the track for Shaftoe Crags. Pass a disused
walled garden on your left and follow the
track up to a gate which leads to the fell.
Pass through and carry on up the cobbled
road to the crags, detouring off to enjoy
the views and explore the crags and the
rock basin known as the Devil's
Punchbowl. (Take care climbing on the
rock; there is a sheer drop to the south.)
The Jacobite Earl of Derwentwater is said
to have sheltered here before being
captured, charged with high treason and
executed on London's Tower Hill in 1716.

Continue on the path to pass Shaftoe

◀ Bolam Lake

Grange, bearing right of the wall. Keep with the wall to reach Salter's Nick, a big gap in the escarpment through which an old drove road passed. During the time of the Salt Tax it was used by smugglers who usually returned from their journeys north with illicit whisky. The remains of Iron Age and Romano-British settlements can be seen on top of the crags.

Turn right after the Nick on the path which crosses the moorland and meadow to reach a rough road which eventually leads back to Bolam West Houses. Bear right at the road and head back towards Bolam Lake. Carry on down the road to the car park you started from or take a stroll around the lake first by entering the woods at the West Woods car park and following the signposts.

Red squirrels, badgers, foxes and roe deer can all be seen in the woodland around the man-made lake, which was designed by Tyneside architect John Dobson for the owner of Bolam House in 1816. More recently there were a number of sightings of a Yeti-type creature here in 2000; so look out for big footprints in the undergrowth on your way back to the start.

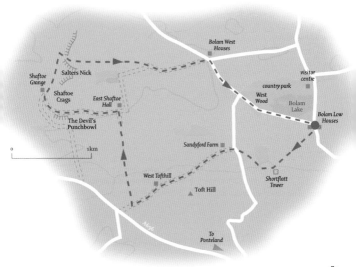

Morpeth loops

**Distance 6km Time 2 hours
Terrain riverside and woodland tracks,
paths and pavements with some steps
and a number of gates. Steady winding
climb up to the castle Map OS Explorer
325 Access trains to Morpeth from
Newcastle and Edinburgh. Buses from
Newcastle and Berwick**

**This circular riverside walk takes you
past the sparse ruins of a once-important
Cistercian Abbey by the banks of the
Wansbeck and up to Morpeth Castle.**

Start out from the old clocktower in
Morpeth town centre and head down to
Oldgate Bridge. As you pass the Royal
Mail sorting office and Catholic Church,
the next red brick building is Collingwood
House, former home of the great British
naval hero Admiral Lord Collingwood.

Turn right after the bridge and pass the
Bakehouse Stepping Stones, following the
signposts for Lady's Walk and
Newminster Abbey. Pass the metal
Skinnery Bridge and continue along the
signed trail around the bend of the River
Wansbeck. Follow the path to the right as
it goes downhill and join the road as it
swings around to the left. Take care on
the roadside by the stone bridge as you
head straight on to the wooden sign for
Mitford and Kirkhill.

The path runs down a quiet side road
past Monk's Lodge House with the sparse
remains of Newminster Abbey on
privately-owned land to your left.
Founded by Ranulf de Merley, Lord of
Morpeth, in 1138, Newminster was once a
very important abbey which held lands all
the way up to the Scottish border.

Carry on to reach a kissing gate,
following the yellow waymarked footpath.
The path turns left just before a second
gate, signed for Kirkhill. Go through the
wooden gate by the tree, heading up the
woodland track to a second kissing gate

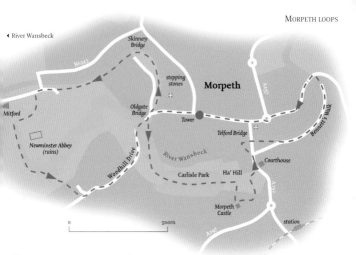

◄ River Wansbeck

Skinnery
Bridge

B6343

stepping
stones

Morpeth

Oldgate
Bridge

Mitford

Tower

Newminster Abbey
(ruins)

Telford Bridge

Bennett's Walk

Woodhill Drive

River Wansbeck

Courthouse

Carlisle Park   Ha' Hill

Morpeth
Castle

station

0   500m

halfway up the field. Continue uphill until it levels off into more trees. Take the right fork in the track and go through another kissing gate, following the track by the treeline past the housing estate and out onto the road.

Bear left past Downing Drive and follow the road down towards Oldgate Bridge. Turn right before the bridge onto the riverside path into Carlisle Park and continue past the bowling green and tennis courts. As you reach the small cottage just past the tennis courts, turn right and head up the path by Ha' Hill, the site of an 11th-century motte and bailey castle. This huge earthwork was created by William de Merley, First Baron of Morpeth, in 1080.

Take the path into the gardens and follow the right path into Postern Woods, swinging around the base of Ha' Hill, then left over the burn and sharply right up the

hill to reach Morpeth Castle. In 1516, Margaret Tudor, the widow of King James IV of Scotland, spent four months here taking refuge from her enemies over the border.

Walk down to the entrance of Carlisle Park opposite the old Court House and continue into Castle Square. Go past the Waterford Lodge and turn right at the Joiners Arms before taking another right just before the footbridge to pass under the Telford Bridge on the riverside path.

Climb the steps and continue along the high path of Bennett's Walk until you reach the blue metal footbridge. Cross the river here and follow the road up Gas House Lane, past the ambulance station, following the pavement to St George's United Reformed Church. Cross at the traffic lights and follow the main street back up to the clocktower.

Plessey Woods

Distance 2km **Time** 1 hour
Terrain compacted woodland and
riverside trails with some steps
Map OS Explorer 316 **Access** Arriva bus
(43) from Morpeth, Newcastle or
Cramlington (no Sunday service); get off
at Hartford Bridge. Car park (pay and
display) at the visitor centre

**Popular with dog walkers and strollers
alike, Plessey Woods Country Park is a
pleasant rural idyll with over 100 acres of
meadow and parkland. Close to the large
towns of Bedlington and Cramlington, it
is easily reached by public transport.**

Plessey Woods take their name from
John de Plessey, who was granted
permission to use timber from the
woodland to build a mill in the 13th
century. Coal was mined here from the
mid-17th century to the early 19th century

and also sandstone which was used in
many local buildings, and, so it is said,
the Houses of Parliament.

From the pay and display car park take
the path to the visitor centre and follow
the wooden signpost for the riverside.

The trail swings left over a footbridge
and continues on into the woodland. You
can easily forget that you are so near to
urban centres as you follow the leafy path
with birdsong in your ears.

Take the left track at the fork signed for
Pegwhistle Burn Quarry Woods and
follow it down through the trees, crossing
the burn at the footbridge.

Continue to your right, following the
burn, climbing up and down some
wooden steps, and go straight ahead at
the blue waymarker. Pass the old quarry
rockface and continue on the path as it
swings to the left and crosses the burn at

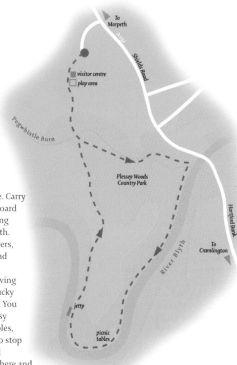

◂ On the River Blyth

another wooden bridge. Carry on to an information board and Valley Wood running alongside the River Blyth.

Look out for kingfishers, dippers, mute swans and heron as you carry on alongside the slow-moving river; if you are really lucky you might see an otter. You eventually reach a grassy clearing with picnic tables, which is a great place to stop for lunch. There are red squirrels in the woods here and several feeders – although the shy little creatures are more reluctant to come out at busy times when more dogs are being walked. Roe deer, stoats, foxes, rabbits and hare are also commonly seen in the surrounding meadowland.

The river leads you round past a wooden jetty popular with anglers – go up the steps, keeping to the low riverside path. Further on, take the steps up to your right until you reach the wooden sign for the visitor centre. Follow this to reach a kissing gate; from here take the broad path to your left which leads back around to the Pegwhistle Burn sign, where you retrace you steps to the visitor centre.

Druridge Bay

Distance 9km **Time** 2 hours 30 (one way)
Terrain roadside pavements, sandy
beaches and dune tracks **Map** OS Explorer
325 **Access** buses to Cresswell from
Ashington/Newbiggin; car parking at
Cresswell Beach

**This out-and-back beach walk follows
the start of the Northumberland Coast
Path which runs for 103km (64 miles)
from Cresswell, at the southern end
of Druridge Bay, right up to Berwick-
upon-Tweed.**

The small village of Cresswell is home
to only 200 people, but two nearby
caravan parks mean that the population
swells in the summer. The 14th-century
Cresswell Tower, hiding in the trees above
the village, was the medieval home of the
Cresswell family.

From the official Coast Path start point
in the village, walk down the sandy path
and concrete steps onto the beach and
turn left, heading north towards Amble
and Coquet Island.

Backed by high dunes, the officially
designated 'Heritage Coast' of Druridge
Bay arcs around in an 11km-long sweep of
golden sand from The Scars, the rocks
which protect Cresswell from the sea, to
Hauxley to the north. South of Cresswell
the coastline is rockier and black with
coals; the horses tethered up on the
dunes around here can sometimes be
seen pulling carts used to gather it up.

Carry on north up the beach until the
dunes on your left become rocky; come
up off the sand here and through the
dunes to the road and carry on heading
north. The dunes here are managed by
the National Trust.

The views to your left pan over rolling
green countryside to the hills at
Simonside and beyond to the Cheviots.
This stretch of coastline was considered
particularly vulnerable to a beach attack

during the Second World War and, as well as pillboxes and anti-tank blocks, there are other defensive points around here cleverly disguised in old farm buildings and under walls.

Druridge Pools Nature Reserve, reclaimed from open-cast mining activity, is on your left as you carry on. The ponds and wetland here attract a great variety of wintering and passing birds. After a short distance you can detour left just past the trees and continue along the path over marshland to visit the bird observation hut.

A further short detour can be made here to visit the ruins of a Dower House, which was first built as a Preceptory of the Kights Hospitallers, at Low Chibburn. To get there look out for a signposted path heading inland which crosses several stiles and fields. Return by the same way.

Back at the dunes, you can carry on heading north by the road or make your way back to the beach at the access points. Staying on the road you will come to the East Chevington Nature Reserve; two lakes fringed with reedbeds which attract whooper swan, grasshopper warbler and greylag and pink-footed geese.

Further up the road, Druridge Bay Country Park has a visitor centre with a café; if you have the energy there are plenty more trails around the park and Ladyburn Lake which you can explore before returning by the road or beach to the start.

Ashington to Newbiggin-by-the-Sea

Distance 7km Time 2 hours
Terrain compacted park trails, footpaths
and roadside pavements; all-terrain
buggy and wheelchair friendly
Map OS Explorer 325 Access regular
buses to Ashington from Morpeth
and Newcastle

Explore Northumberland's mining
heritage as you make your way through
Queen Elizabeth II Country Park, once the
site of one of the largest colliery slag
heaps in Europe, to reach the North Sea
at Newbiggin-by-the-Sea.

Turn right from Ashington bus station
and right again at the roundabout on the
A197, following the sign for the entrance
to the Queen Elizabeth II Country Park.

Cross the railway line at a safe time and
follow the wooden public footpath
fingerpost into the woods through the

huge old metal bucket at the entrance
to the park.

Continue straight ahead, following the
yellow arrow waymarkers around the lake,
passing a hotel and an old pithead wheel,
a reminder that this was once the heart of
Northumberland's coal mining industry.
Mining here began in 1894 with the first
coal produced in 1901; production ended
in 1981 and the park is now an excellent
example of restored industrial land.

A narrow gauge railway runs along to
your left as you continue round the lake;
follow this to the entrance of the superb
Woodhorn Colliery Museum next to the
old 'headgear' which supported the lift
cables running down into the mine shaft.

At its peak, almost 2000 men worked
the coal seams here and the preserved
colliery buildings, museum exhibits and
the collection of artworks by the 'Pitmen

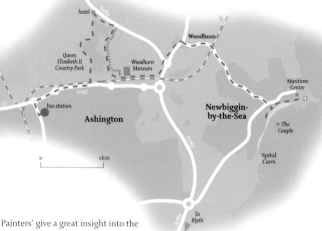

The Couple at Newbiggin

Painters' give a great insight into the industry and the lives and working conditions of miners.

Leaving the museum, turn left and cross the road via the cycle route signed for Woodhorn. Take the path into the trees and on into Woodhorn Village. Cross the road and head left down the pavement, following the sign for Newbiggin. Pass Woodhorn Church on your right and continue under the road flyover. The pavement leads you directly into Newbiggin-by-the-Sea.

Keep bearing south on the pavement down Woodhorn Road, crossing at the school, and on into Newbiggin, turning left at the seafront sign.

Walk through the main shopping street, crossing at the bandstand to reach the seafront promenade. Out to sea, *The Couple*, two five-metre high bronze figures, stand on a huge metal platform keeping a watch over the sea. The sculpture was created by Sean Henry and installed in 2007.

Walking north up the wide promenade takes you to Church Point and St Bartholemew's Church, one of the oldest places of worship in Northumberland – the monks of Lindisfarne built a chapel here to use on their journeys to and from Tynemouth Priory and Whitby. The nearby Newbiggin Maritime Centre is also worth a visit before you catch the bus back to Ashington; as well as various interesting displays, the café overlooks the sea and serves toasted stotties.

Index